# Preface

You know something that others should know. But you may not know how to share that something — that idea, those feelings — with others in print. And even if you write like Shakespeare (or Sandburg) what you have to say won't be published until you can get an editor to give you the nod.

Five years back I wrote *The Query Book* to help you, and others like you, bridge the gap of getting into print, as professionals do, with query letters. Query letters are the difference between amateurs and professionals in the writing world. A well written query is almost negotiable tender.

So this book contains much of what that book said about queries, with more examples and a few, modest changes. I also asked editors from a wide variety of publications to share their ideas about queries, and those comments are included, where appropriate. You'll see that there's not much difference between what I'm writing and what they're wanting.

*The Query Book* was incomplete. It only told you how to sell before you write, with queries. It didn't show you the tools you need to sell once a manuscript is written, or how to repeatedly resell an article already in print.

So this text talks about the second set of tools all successful writers need: cover letters. It shows how they differ from queries, when they are used, what they look like, and why they are sent in some cases and not in others. Ten examples show the usual range of cover letters needed. Beyond that, your own wit and skill will carry you through.

You see, if you're smart and literate enough to write copy sufficiently good to be printed, it won't take you long to catch on to querying, then following up, when needed, with cover letters. But they aren't magic. They don't substitute for clear thought, tight editing, and persistence. They do let you compete in the writing world like a professional from the first day, though, and they'll keep you earning regularly and reliably until you put your pen to rest.

When I wrote the first edition of this book I had been in print 350 times. Since then I've had about 600 more items in print. It's not the writing that makes the difference. My writing is no better than yours. It's the way I market. It's the fact that I do precisely what I'm telling you how to do on these pages. And if it works for me, friend, it will work for you!

As I said, there's no magic to writing. It's hard work. But the rewards far outweigh the toil and testing. And anyway, we need to know what you have to say. You're important and it's important. So get reading, then get writing. We'll see you soon in print.

# Dedication

To Judy, as with *The Query Book*, again for her patience and help;

To Shannon, still waiting for the racing car from the earnings of that book, who has lovingly settled for an aging Pinto, and

To Kim, hope reigning eternal, who continues to hold out for faster wheels — and thinks, hopes, this one will be it!

# Contents

# PART ONE

## What This Book Is All About

# 1

# The Letters, The Editor, You, Selling, and Time

You want to write for a living? Great! The writing part is easy enough — you've been doing it since you were a kid.

Just think of how many times you've read something in print and said, "I can write better than that!"

You probably can, or soon could with practice.

But could you do it regularly? Could you live on that income? It's the "for a living" part that separates the wishers from the doers. And that depends upon how you use your time.

For years I taught a class called "How to Sell 75% of Your Freelance Writing"; now I offer that material as a seminar and through a book by the same name. The title is a mouthful but it's right on target. If you sell much less than 75% of what you write you can't make it professionally, or for a living.

This book will guide you through the two most important elements of selling your writing.

First it will discuss the querying process. It will cover the few and scattered points made in other literature about querying, and add substantially to them. Sample query letters are also included, in part to make up for their scarcity elsewhere.

It will also show you how and when to write cover letters, with examples. That is, it will cover the two key marketing tools that all writers need to know and use: queries, sent before you write the copy, and cover letters, which accompany copy already written.

# The Query Letter

A query letter, in a sentence, is a letter sent to an editor asking if he/she would be interested in (buying) an article about ... But it isn't quite that simple.

How long should the letter be? What must it contain, and what should it never say? To whom should it be sent? When will that person reply? What happens if they don't? Why not query by phone? And isn't it far more efficient to send the same letter to a dozen editors, then write for the one who promises to pay the most?

# The Cover Letter

A cover letter accompanies a manuscript or copy. It's usually short and to the point: is the editor interested in using the material attached? Yet again it's not that simple.

Why is the copy being sent? Why isn't the sender querying? Has it been in print before? Are photos available? What rights are being offered? What are the author's qualifications? And more.

In both cases there is a need for a general grasp of the relationship between the letter, the editor, you (the writer), a professional selling process, and time. Such an understanding will put the most important element — writing — into its proper perspective.

# What You Really Sell

What you sell in print is time. The time it takes you to think up something to write about that others want to read, test the topic to see that it can be written about, identify markets, find an interested editor, complete the research, write, edit, submit, sell, and resell.

Those who can do this quickly and well will get the biggest rewards: fortune and fame. The fortune will be modest, at least at the outset. The fame will be even more modest. The key word is "quickly." If you don't do every aspect of this process well, you simply won't be in print.

Thus what you want to do is what every professional does: find the fastest and most efficient way to reduce time-taking risks and to increase the profitability of every moment used. That's where query and cover letters fit in. Without them, you are reduced to groping in the unknown, wandering days and months trying to match ideas, words, and hope to print dollars.

With them, you zero in on markets and reduce the groping and wandering. The crucial tool is the query. Then you multiply one sale into many with the cover letter.

So let's focus primarily on the query here, mentioning the cover letter only when it is appropriate now, so we can concentrate more fully on it later.

# How To Prepare and Market Articles That Sell

When you write an article for a magazine you can either write the copy and send it to the editor, as many novices do, or you can ask the editor first if he/she would be interested in reading/using the article when written. Professionals do the latter, though there are exceptions, which I will explain later.

The first approach assumes either that you have infinite time and extraordinary skills to turn out many, many super articles or you are psychic, and thus know what each editor needs. Unless the latter is true, in which case you'd be far richer simply selling that knowledge to other writers, you will wind up spending 90% of your time writing, typing, editing, and rewriting to sell maybe 5% or 10% of what you produce.

That's foolish. Professionals can't survive on publishing's meager returns unless they sell at least 75% of their work — and most easily top 100%, with simultaneous submissions and reprints. They write a one-page letter, a query, and only write the article when the editor gives them a positive, "let-me-see-it" response. Then they resell the sold item, through cover letters, time and time again.

This process is the step-by-step theme of my recent book, *How To Sell 75% of Your Freelance Writing*. Query letters, then cover letters, are the tools that distinguish amateurs from professionals and make that 75% selling ratio possible.

The book you are reading expands mightily the discussion and presentation, through examples, of each of those elements.

Yet to put query and cover letters into perspective, let me borrow a 15-step guide from *How To Sell 75% of Your Freelance Writing*:

(1.) In one sentence, what is the subject of the article you want to write and sell?

(2.) Who would benefit from reading your article? Who would be most interested? What kinds of readers would select your specific subject from a variety of choices? Rank all of those potential readers in order with those who would derive the most benefits first.

(3.) Which publications do these readers buy and read? Prepare a market list of those publications that are the most likely to buy your manuscript.

(4.) In addition to the publications checked in (3.), it is necessary to review the broader publishing field for articles similar or identical to yours. Therefore, you must check both the *Reader's Guide to Periodical Literature* and the specific subject indexes for at least three previous years, then

    (a) list the articles that are closest to your subject, in order with the most similar first: subject, author, title, publication, page reference, length, and when they appeared. Where the subjects appear to be very similar, how does yours differ?

    (b) cross-check newspaper indexes for the past three years and provide the same information.

(5.) Have the publications listed in (3. and 4.) printed articles within the past three years that are similar to the one you propose?

(6.) After each publication note the name of the person you should contact (editor, managing editor, etc.), with title and address. Then provide the following information about each publication:
    (a) does it pay on acceptance or publication?
    (b) how much does it pay for articles as long as yours?
    (c) does it prefer a query or a direct submission?
    (d) how often is it published?
    (e) what percentage of it is written by freelancers?
    (f) what is its preferred manuscript length?
    (g) is any other information provided that will affect its placement on your list?

(7.) Now rank your market list in priority order, based on when the buyers pay (acceptance/publication), how much, the frequency of publication, and the percentage of freelance material used per issue.

(8.) Read the latest issues of your target publication, front to back. Select the articles that are the most similar, in form if not topic, to the piece you will prepare. Outline each article. Write out the lead and conclusion of each, by hand. Attempt to identify the publication's readers by age, sex, occupation, income range, education, residence, and other pertinent factors.

(9.) To verify the availability of resource information
    (a) read as many of the articles in (5.) as necessary or possible, then list the sources of information found in each,
    (b) go to the library and consult the card catalog and list books to which you will refer for factual information: title, author, call number, date of publication, and
    (c) list the human resources you should consult for additional information and quotes, working with the reference librarian for information that you do not already have: their names, positions and current affiliations (if related to the topic), academic titles and degrees (if relevant), and reasons for their being consulted.

(10.) From the researched and specific target publication information gathered, select the material needed to write a professional query letter. Verify its accuracy.

(11.) Write a selling query letter to an editor of your target publication. If you do not receive a positive reply, write a query letter to the editor of the next publication on your list, and so on, one editor at a time, until an editor does respond positively. Repeat as much of (9.) as necessary for each new publication queried.

(12.) When you receive that positive response to your query, plan your article to determine what is still needed for its completion.

(13.) Complete the needed research.

(14.) Write the manuscript in final draft form. Include, on separate paper, at least five additional, different leads.

(15.) Select the best lead, edit the draft, type a final manuscript (keeping a copy), and mail it, with illustrations (if available and needed), to the editor of your target publication.

Ten of the fifteen steps *precede* the query letter. You must first find something to write about, decide whether it's feasible to complete an article about that topic, and whether there are markets with readers eager for your information.

Then you query. You send a letter to the editor of the most likely publication. If you get a negative reply, you try the second editor, and down the list, one at a time, until a publishing genius recognizes your talents and a gripping topic and says "yes, I'll look at it!" Only then do you fully research, interview, photo, and write.

The details about the querying process are explained in the chapters that follow. Let me add a few more thoughts about the general topics of writing and selling before we look at an actual query letter.

# Writing

Most beginners eager to be in print put too much emphasis on writing skills and pay too little attention to selling, in part because selling is so poorly explained in the books they have at hand.

Yet the actual writing, the formation of phrases and paragraphs around thoughts, is little mystery to a literate person. In fact, if you can wrap four good sentences around a thought, and do that consistently, you can be a selling writer.

Three words are crucial: clarity, brevity, and flow. If you can present an interesting idea clearly and briefly, and your presentation flows smoothly and sensibly, about all that is missing is an interest-grabbing lead, a conclusion, and factual accuracy.

You can read books about each of these elements, and more. Better yet, read the articles in the publications in which you want to appear and focus on each until you see how the writer has treated the subject and why the article is in print.

Writing is like swimming. It takes a bit of practice to coordinate the motions but once you have learned it, you never unlearn it. In both, the more you practice the better you get. In swimming, you may eventually want to study with a master. In writing, you can pick up almost any good reading and learn. The rest is putting the learning on paper.

In summary, if you can write as well as the articles already in print where you want to appear, if your query letter gets you a chance to submit your work for serious consideration by that publication, and your article is then accepted, what more can you ask? Only that it be printed again, by others. Do that enough and you will be writing for a living.

# Selling

Most writers shake in fear of their supposed writing inadequacies. They are shaking for the wrong reason. What they usually can't do is sell. Not that they are incapable of selling either themselves or their copy, they just don't know how. If they did, they'd see that selling would force their writing skills to improve to meet their querying promises.

In principle, selling your writing could not be simpler. You convince an editor hundreds or thousands of miles away that you have an exciting idea his or her magazine needs because it tells the readers something they want to know but don't. What's more, you are the person who should tell them. Finally, the editor can see by the lively, bright, clear, concise prose in your one-page letter that you can write. In fact, all that's missing is the go-ahead and you'll have a blue ribbon manuscript in his/her hands pronto. (The "great piece!" note and check will quickly follow.)

That's what a query letter should do.

You see where the writing fits in. Unless your query is well written, unless it reads as smoothly as the copy in the publication and it convinces the editor that you can present ideas clearly and fully, that editor will not ask to see your manuscript. There are too many other query letters on the editor's desk that do those things to gamble on you. So your query must be written well. Then you must follow it up with a manuscript as good.

In living up to those expectations your writing will either meet the demand or you will not write for a living. Cruel but a fact.

Do you see why I say that selling or marketing is the first and most important step, and that writing follows like an eager and growing puppy, obediently behind?

The responsibility of this book, then, is clear: to show you what a query letter looks like, what it must contain, when and how it is sent, and a multitude of other nuances which could be the difference between not writing for sale at all, writing and selling now and then, or writing for a living.

Then, later, to show how the cover letter extends the life and sales power of an item already written.

We've talked around it. Let's look at an actual query letter in the next chapter, and use that as the basis for answering "what is a query letter?"

---

*"Chances of selling are practically nil without a query."*

John Fink, Editor, *Chicago* Magazine

# PART TWO

## Query Letters For Articles

# 2

# What Is a Query and What Should It Say?

A query, in simplest terms, is a question, an inquiry. For nonfiction freelancers, querying is most often done by a letter built around the phrase "Would you be interested in . . .?" Its purpose is to interest an editor in an idea he or she will want to use in their publication.

Not all queries are made by letter. When they might be better done by phone or in person is discussed later. Those thinking of querying by other, more exotic means are left to their own designs, with the question "why?"

Some elements must appear in every query: what you want the editor to consider, your name, and how you can be contacted. Thus a letter asking for editorial or writer's guidelines, while a good idea before querying, is not a query. Nor is a letter asking an editor what is needed, a letter to avoid because it shows that you have no concept of what a writer should do: provide both ideas and manuscripts.

Also commonly included in query letters are some mention of your published credits, your special preparation or expertise in dealing with the topic, the sources that will be used, perhaps the names of those to be interviewed, the type and quality of illustrations to be submitted with the manuscript, and enough factual material about the topic to convince the editor that readers would benefit from and enjoy reading your article.

Freelancers want to sell their writing, while editors need to buy good copy to fill their pages. The query letter is a timesaver that lets you, the writer, test an idea before having to complete the research, conduct interviews, take photos, and write the manuscript. Instead, you lightly research your idea to see if a full piece can be written about it and whether your thesis can be supported. When you are certain that your article is worth writing and can be written, you write a query letter asking if the editor would be interested in using such an idea/article in his or her publication.

The editor doesn't know at this point whether you have written the article or are about to, and can only assume that if you speak of it as a reality, the manuscript will be delivered as promised.

Based on that assumption, the editor responds, telling you to:

(1.)  mail the manuscript and a check will be sent, now or upon receipt, for its purchase;

(2.)  mail the manuscript on speculation, meaning that if the editor thinks the final piece, once read, can be used, as is or with alterations, a check will follow;

(3.)  wait, usually citing some reason for delaying full consideration of the idea;

(4.)  not send the manuscript, rejecting it with a personal comment or explanation why it can't be used, or

(5.)  not send the manuscript, rejecting it without a personal comment, often on a mass-produced form.

The first — a purchase, sight unseen — is highly unlikely unless you have sold to a market repeatedly or you have a reputation that assures you or your agent some form of advance payment. As unlikely is (3). The fate of newcomers to the writing world is that editors will either pass judgment on their labors before giving them the nod or will turn them down. Good query letters will usually save you from the dehumanizing fate of (5), and will frequently move you from (4) to (2) on your second or subsequent query. The initial idea may be quite logically rejected (the editor has just bought a similar piece, he ran something too much like it last year, etc.), but later queries will benefit from the solid writing of the first as much as by the writer's persistence in breaking into the new market with good writing and good ideas.

Since most freelancers are relative newcomers, this book makes the assumption that a go-ahead or positive reply on speculation, (2) above, is the most favorable response the writer can consistently expect. When that writer has gained the experience and reputation to move into the (1) category, payment before or upon delivery, that writer will probably have slid out of the freelance classification in all but a technical sense.

I make a further assumption that is too optimistic in fact: that every editor giving a go-ahead does so with the full intent of ultimately buying the manuscript if, in final form, it meets the promises of the query. Unfortunately, a few editors respond to almost every query by telling the writer to submit the work on speculation. Almost all of those pieces are later rejected. The only tip-off to those editors comes in the type of go-ahead they send. If it is mass produced or impersonal, beware.

# Subject

Again, the purpose of the query letter is to sell an idea, then a manuscript for publication. The heart of the query letter is that idea. Everything else is secondary. The form most likely to sell the idea will dictate the form the letter takes. If the piece is to be solemn in tone, the query will also be solemn. If the topic is fluffy and fun, the letter should show evidence of the same light joy. Which is not to say that it should be silly and pointless, rather that it must enhance the manuscript's consideration, and sale, by showing your ability to write the piece as you wrote the query.

Too many of my students' query letters fail to show a full grasp of the subject. Often the letters are too short and the facts, too sparse or suspect. One way to assure that the topic is adequately covered is to consider the query letter as a precis or single-page summary of a piece already written, from which the writer must select the "best" order so the editor will know what the piece is about and how it conveys its message. The summary should include the subject and your approach to it, supporting data, the conclusions to be drawn, and the reason why a reader should even care about the topic in the first place, if that isn't obvious.

# Expertise or Preparation

Editors will want to know how you got your facts, if they are reliable and accurate, and how well you know the field.

This is particularly important when writing for specialized journals. Editors in the medical field aren't waiting for a piece from a layman who thinks that maybe canker sores will be cured someday. However, they would be interested in cures, methods of treatment, or scientific studies on the causes and treatments of similar viral problems here or abroad. You needn't be a doctor or a scientist. All the editors ask is that you have a firm understanding of the subject and can cite sources and studies that are, as I said, reliable and accurate — and verifiable.

Should you mention your academic background? Only if (1) that background gives you special insight into the topic, (2) it provides you with a unique understanding of the topic, (3) you are writing about academia, or (4) you are writing to academics.

Two editor friends laughed when I asked how they would respond to a list of earned degrees in a query letter. Their replies were the same: "That's fine, but can the person write? And can the reader believe what that person says?"

# Previous Publications

If you have none, say nothing. If you have a few and they fall into the church bulletin and hometown newspaper category, silence is again the best policy — unless that paper serves a major city. Mention previous publications only if they are impressive. If the query letter itself shouts "professional," their absence won't be noted. If the query letter proves that you are a beginner, 100 publications in alphabetical order won't make much difference. They won't be believed.

If I've sold to a publication before, I'd naturally mention it, particularly if another editor reigned during the earlier sale. Only if I wish to show an editor that I've worked a wide range of fields when I'm proposing a subject with particularly broad appeal will I give a more extensive list, and that never more than 10 or 12.

There is a temptation for beginners to puff their credits — to raise a real three to a fictitious 33 — by citing magazines they wish they had sold to. A foolish game, really. You will be judged on the manuscript prepared in response to a query go-ahead, and if it shows too little writing skill, not only will the piece be rejected, the editor will wonder how you could have sold so often before. Your name will stick, negatively, and it may well be harder for you to break into print with that editor the next time around. Even worse, what if the editor asks to see specific examples of your previous work?

Sometimes a market write-up does request tearsheets or samples of earlier published work. An editor occasionally makes the same request after reading a query. Try to find examples as close to the editor's publication as you can, without too much regard to date, although I always include the most recent piece I have in print too. If you have very few sales but examples are asked for, send photocopies of what you do have.

# Illustrations

These include photographs, slides, drawings, maps, charts, and other items used to illustrate your manuscript.

Some pieces particularly require illustrations. If you are trying to sell a bloodracer called "How I Caught A 400-pound *Pirarucú*," you had better have more than one dim slide showing you in an Amazonian setting with a gar-like, tongued fish larger than yourself. Likewise, a story about hiking the lost trail across the Andean *páramo* had better come with slides or photos of a trail devoid of Baby Ruth wrappers in a setting convincingly Ecuadorian.

The number of photos and slides you can provide will interest the editor, as will their size and quality. Unless it is germane to the story, who took them is less important than that they were taken. Frequently

I am writing in one part of California and trustworthy photographer friends are elsewhere snapping shots for me. A graphics colleague often provides comical drawings to illustrate my humor pieces, enlarging markets for both of us.

Should you send illustrations with the query letter? I don't because they can get lost en route or go astray at the destination. Mention what you can provide in the query, then wait until the editor requests samples.

With black and whites I have a proof sheet made, instead of prints. I cut out the best shots from the proof paper and mount them presentably on a regular sheet of paper, like stamps in an album, with double-stick tape or rolled tape on the back. Each shot is numbered below, and a caption sheet accompanies each page of b/w proofs explaining the shots by number. If the editor is interested in particular shots, I send the corresponding negatives or a 5 x 7 or 8 x 10 print, depending upon that editor's request or ability to make the prints in-house.

If the editor wants slides, my action is based on the value of the shots. If I have plenty of slides and these aren't particularly valuable, I send originals, each with my name and address. A caption sheet accompanies the slides, explaining each.

But if the slides are once-in-a-lifetime shots, I have copies made of the best and send the copies in a plastic holder for the editor's selection. The editor indicates which is needed, returning all of the duplicates. Then I send the chosen few, the originals, in the same kind of plastic holder, heavily insured. The system is cumbersome but it works. I've never lost a slide or a client.

---

*"If a query does its job, I have a good idea what the article will be like and the chances of its being rejected are almost nil. But a query to do its job must give me a good idea of how the subject will be covered, how well the writer uses the language, and how much editing I will have to do on the manuscript."*

Bill Sonneborn, Editor, *Michiana* Magazine, of *The South Bend Tribune*

# 3

# A Sample Query Letter

We have talked around and about query letters. It's time we read one!

The letter that follows, as all others in this book, was actually sent to an editor. In most cases the letters are precisely as written; in a few (mainly cover letters) they are reconstructed from notes when originals were lost or never kept. With one major exception: I have changed the editors/publications/addresses and sometimes the names of the people in the letters. The reason is sad but simple: a few who saw the actual names in the first edition of this book or in seminar materials bothered those mentioned!

## The Purpose of This Letter

It tells Allen Hearty that I have information about a person his readers would like to know, and that I'd like to write an article about that person.

I could have written a manuscript instead of the query letter. Hearty would have been able to see how I treated Kurt Gluck, how much fishing was included in the text, and the ratio of dialog to anecdote and straight narrative. I might even have sent 35mm color slides along so he could see the whole package at once.

It might have taken me five to ten hours to complete some back-up research, write the copy (and rewrite and edit the writing), type the final draft, and prepare the slides and captions. That presumes that I

## Query Example #1

123 Main Street
Carpinteria, CA 93013
(805) 123-4567
Month 1, Year

Mr. Allen Hearty
Editor, Fishing Today
808 Third Street
New York, NY 10000

Dear Mr. Hearty:

Kurt Gluck is a quiet hero, a soft-spoken legend poking into the Amazon backlands. Never mind that he's the best known guide from Belem to Iquitos. The other guides think he's crazy.

At 63, he's the last of a vanishing breed of fighters holding off the commercial hacks at the 1,000-mile inland mecca of Manaus, famous for lost rubber riches and modern-day free port booty. Kurt lives on a back street and is better known in Tokyo, Munich, and Miami Beach than in Brazil.

For $30 a day, to the rich or poor, he will fill his 8-hp motor with gas, point his canoe into the rushing furos of the poorly tamed Rio Negro, and enter his beloved wilds. Kurt doesn't hunt, except to survive. He'd rather fish, and few know a greater thrill than to paddle silently at his side in a shaded pool to the curious scrutiny of cheiro monkeys and irridescent morpho butterflies, to jolt at the arm-wrenching bite of the fierce tucunares, the clamp-jawed tiger piranhas, or even the boat-spilling pirarucus, largest freshwater fish in the world.

Gluck's a tough, gnarled old warrior in love with nature who laughs at stories of man-eating piranha, calling them 99% myth. He swims with pink dolphin, pulls teeth, and has put most of his children through medical school.

I've just returned from Brazil where I went to college some years back. I've been in print in magazines 350 times since, and can provide 50 good to excellent 35mm slides of Kurt and fishing near Lake Janauari, an hour from Manaus. Are Fishing Today readers ready to share some of this Brazilian adventure and joy, Mr. Hearty?

Gordon Burgett

was familiar with *Fishing Today*, had closely studied the type of material it used, and had a sense of what its readers found interesting.

Instead, the query took 20 minutes to write, perhaps another 20 to rewrite and edit — at most an hour from inception to mailing.

The key point is that Hearty rejected the query, with kind words and encouragement about future ideas, etc. I lost one-fifth to one-tenth the time I would have had I written and sent the manuscript instead of a query. And I wasn't stuck with a written manuscript that would have had to be rewritten for the next submission.

Instead, I had a rejection letter and my copy of the query. I lamented the first, then read the second, turned to my list for another market, and had a new query in the mail within 30 minutes. Two weeks later the story was sold! Or at least I had a go-ahead, with some very specific directions about how the biographical piece was to be slanted to interest the second magazine's readers. I wrote it to match those directions, then sold it. Had I just sent the already written manuscript (presuming I had written one for Hearty instead of querying), it would have been rejected again.

The point is obvious. Why write a manuscript when in the same length of time you can write a dozen query letters? When an editor gives you the green light, then you write the article directly for that magazine's readers and editor, who knows it is coming and has it already pencilled in for a future edition, if it meets the publication's standards.

## There's More Than Time Involved...

By pencilling in your topic the editor is involved in the process. He or she has been in your shoes, knows what a writer must do, and is now psychologically part of your doing it. The editor has a vested interest in your manuscript when it arrives. By giving you the go-ahead, by taking your query promise and mentally fitting it into a future issue, the editor has become to a small degree, at least in spirit, your co-author.

Therefore, that editor is far less liable to reject your submission — and far more likely to cheer a job very well done! Only two things are guaranteed to turn that spirit against you: sending in something other than what your query promised or submitting a manuscript that is far below professional level.

The point? Reread your query more than once when you write your final manuscript and stick to it! Then make your prose hum. Work, write, edit, move the words around, write again — until your article reads like the best in the last edition of *Fishing Today*.

Consider the difference between the reception your copy receives and a manuscript some beginner sends in, completely written, unexpected, about a topic new to the editor. Which is Allen Hearty most likely to buy?

You see, editors expect query letters, not manuscripts. Professionals send queries; amateurs don't — until they start acting like professionals. By sending queries.

# Why This Query Is Written As It Is

*Fishing Today* is a serious magazine little given to humor. It considers fishing less a hobby or restful avocation than a contest between man and all aquatic life. It's pro-conservation, as that pertains to water and fish, but nonetheless seems intent upon showing the reader how to catch the limit every time out. Its one concession: it constantly seeks exciting, new locations for its articles. Its greatest blessing? It pays $1,000 for 1,800 words, photos extra! Any wonder why it was first on my market list?

The query takes into consideration all of the above.

## Subject:

The letter has one subject, Kurt Gluck, and one approach, serious and straightforward. The primary link to the magazine is fishing, Kurt's favorite activity. Prominent in the query are types of fish, fishing locales, water, and canoes. The rest of the letter fleshes Kurt out, so we know what he is like and why we should care about him. It also tells why I should write the piece.

Some things aren't said. What is a person with a name like Kurt Gluck doing in Brazil? Where's he from? What's his background? Could he be a hiding Nazi? (He's not!) And a dozen more questions, but in the limited space of one page they aren't worth answering. Select only those facts that promote your purpose: to sell an idea, and a manuscript, to the editor. You can answer the other questions in the article.

## Expertise or Preparation:

My expertise is scarcely mentioned in the *Fishing Today* query. In summary, it says (or implies) that I've been to Brazil recently, attended college there, took photos of Kurt and fishing on a lake near the Amazon River, and I have information about Gluck.

Hopefully you didn't notice that I know so little about fishing I can't tell which end of the beast bites. Or that I've never actually fished with Gluck. Neither is important, frankly, because if I get the go-ahead from Hearty, I will learn what I need to know and will interview others who have fished with the likeable Bavarian.

Remember, be honest but say only what best serves your purpose. If you got the impression that we spent weeks harpooning minnows on the tributaries, I'm sorry. That's what good writing can do! Hearty may have guessed, since he said no. But if he had said yes, he would never have known in the final manuscript. I've raised his expectations and must now live up to them. In print we'd net minnows and harpoon *pirarucús*.

I have four degrees centered on Latin America, particularly Brazil, but they aren't mentioned, and barely referred to, in this query. What would be the purpose?

## Previous Publications:

Should I list my publications? Should I list 100? or 200? Why would I? The editor is interested in one thing: can I give him good copy? I limit myself to noting the number of times I've been in print in magazines at that time. Sometimes I list a few publications similar to the editor's that I am querying to show that I've worked the field. (When writing *Fishing Today*, of the then 350 items in print not a one had been sold to a fishing magazine, so I simply cited the number.)

**Illustrations:**

The half-sentence about illustrations in the query could be the difference between a sale or a rejection. It talks about "50 good to excellent 35mm slides of Kurt and fishing near Lake Janauari." As often as not with foreign settings, where photos are critical, the editor will ask to see them before giving a go-ahead.

———————

Let's explore the topic of queries a bit more before reviewing another letter. For example, when should you query?

———————

*"The truth is, most query letters aren't at all promising. They don't convey a sense of the writer's writing style or personal voice; they aren't about an interesting angle on a subject; they aren't accompanied by clips that demonstrate the writer's track record. I think query letters are best written with the potential reader of the piece in mind — not its editor. A good editor should be able to spot what would appeal to his or her readers. Just compose the first two or three paragraphs as if you're talking directly to the reader, then let the editor know why you're the person to write the story."*

John Stoltenberg, Managing Editor, *Essence* Magazine

# 4

# When Should You Query?

**N**ot all writing sales come from query letters, nor does one query for all sales. To help see where querying fits into the selling process we will use the diagram that follows, called "The Mechanics of Getting Into Print." It is based on the 15-step guide we have read, but focusses primarily on the steps taken at and after the query or copy is sent.

The process begins with an idea and ends with the idea appearing in print, making you rich and renowned. There are hurdles, however, between the idea and the ideal.

Since we will explain how query and cover letters follow this process throughout the rest of this book, let's briefly describe the diagram.

Path A is for queried items where a query letter follows the feasibility study. It is mailed to the editor, who responds positively (to which you complete and submit the copy) or negatively (to which you query the next editor on your market list). If the editor buys your copy, after responding positively to your query, you appear in print — at least once!

Path B is for direct submissions where, instead of querying, you write and submit the copy from the outset. Again, the editor either accepts or rejects that copy. If rejected, send it to another editor (or editors, if simultaneously submitted). If bought, *voilá*.

# THE MECHANICS OF GETTING INTO PRINT

**QUERIED SUBMISSIONS**

Path A

1. Complete Feasibility Study
2. Mail completed query letter

EDITOR → no

**DIRECT SUBMISSIONS**

Path B

1. Prepare a market list
2. Prepare, mail manuscript(s)

EDITOR → no

1. Complete research
2. Prepare and submit manuscript
3. (Send visuals, if requested)

IDEA

EDITOR

APPEARS IN PRINT — REWRITE — REPRINT

Path **A** is for most nonfiction articles and books; includes humorous (where humor is the style rather than purpose).

Path **B** is for simultaneous submissions as well as fiction, fillers, and humor (where humor is the purpose).

# 5

# A Second Query Letter

et's look at an actual second query letter, with the original names and all, that is far different in form and purpose from that lauding Kurt Gluck, then follow it, hypothetically, through the steps just mentioned.

While devouring a then recent best seller I got a great idea. "Would you be interested in . . . ?" are the magic querying words, and since the thriller was called *The Book of Lists*, I wrote the editors asking "would they be interested in a list"!

Sound balmy, like trying to sell virtue to a paragon? It would if the Wallace (Wallechinsky) family (father Irving, son David, daughter Any) hadn't asked at the end of the book's forward (p.xx) for us not to "be listless . . . (to) join in" and send them lists for the next edition.

Normally I wouldn't respond to their bid for contributors since I imagine that while they pay for items used, it isn't much. The time spent hunting for lists they missed or trying to compile new ones wouldn't be profitable, and I'm not courting penury by intent.

Alas, I did happen to have two facts stored in a reserve lobe that would take no time at all to develop. It seems that I'd written a children's nonfiction article about "The Seven Kings of the Americas," which was a list in itself, plus a fact about one of those kings fit perfectly into another list that *The Book of Lists* contained.

(Some will ask if it is ethical to use the names of the seven kings, and facts about them, again since I already sold an article in which that appeared. Of course. The magazine didn't buy exclusive rights to the facts, just the copy in which those facts were used. Said in another way, you don't sell ideas, just the specific way in which those ideas are presented.)

# Query Example #2

123 Main Street
Carpinteria, CA 93013
(805) 123-4567
Month 1, Year

Mr. David Wallechinsky
Mr. Irving Wallace
Ms Amy Wallace
The Book of Lists
P.O. Box 49328
Los Angeles, CA 90046

Dear David, Irving, and Amy:

I bought The Book of Lists for the family for Christmas and have
scarcely let them see it since!   The kids homed in like pigeons to the
areas touching on sex.   I know because they left fingerprints and food
stains before I got there.   The entire tome is delightful.

Your readers might enjoy another list I could send you: The Seven
Kings of the Americas, the subject of an article I sold to a juvenile
magazine.   All seven were legitimate rulers of nations we know: three
from Haiti, two from Brazil, and two from Mexico.   Three were
related; three were black, one was mixed, three were from royal
European stock.   Four were killed in their countries, two died in exile,
another died of old age after spending years abroad (part in the U.S.),
deposed.   All ruled during the last century.   Sources provided, of
course.

Would you like the list of the seven prepared in the manner of "10
Unexplored Areas of the World" or "15 Islands for Sale," that is, with
the names and some interesting bio data?

Incidentally, the first of the seven kings, Jean-Jacques Dessalines of
Haiti, might also be listed in the "9 Most Unusual Monuments in the
World," (p. 138), for, like Jose Olmedo, a statue stands in his honor in
a park in Port-au-Prince, Haiti.   Mind you, Dessalines not only hated
whites, he butchered them with glee.   So imagine his chagrin should he
discover that the group buying the statue ran out of funds and could
only find a secondhand reject from a Central American country of a
deposed ruler -- who was white!

Please let me know if either the list or the item about Jean-Jacques is
worth preparing.   Best wishes to all of you.

Gordon Lee Burgett

So, never one to let unearthed facts get reburied unprofitably, I took 15 minutes to write a query to (1) make the editors aware that the information exists, (2) set up a potential sale, and (3) save me from having to compile an actual list without knowing the preferred format.

I query because if the Wallaces are interested they will tell me how they want the information sent. Then I can pluck the old facts from my files, type the copy at one sitting, package and mail it, and wait for the check. In the meantime, the idea is out of my mind and in their hands. I am free to do other things, like sending queries to higher paying markets. If Irving and his kids reply with a "no, thanks," I've lost 15 minutes and a few pennies in stamps. If they want the data, I will reread my copy of the query, match the facts to their directions, and respond promptly.

The system maximizes time-use efficiency and spells success. Enough good ideas well presented will bring you "let-me-see-it" or "go-ahead" replies, and eventually, money in the bank. Your bank.

# Notes about the Query

A touch of humor as an opener, then a deservedly kind work about *The Book of Lists*. Down to business: I have a potential list and a fact to add to the "9 Most Unusual Monuments in the World" list; they should let me know if they want either prepared for their next edition. The rest of the letter makes the items I can provide more interesting or more desirable.

The query shows that I have read their book and am familiar with the kind of material a follow-up might contain. Also, that I know the material I'm offering for sale well enough to have written about it for print. I suggest a format but leave the choice to them.

There's a minor point worth noting: I haven't mentioned all of the material that I want to sell in the query letter. Six of the seven kings are unnamed; the source of the Dessalines fact isn't cited. I can't prevent the editors from digging up the missing elements, but I can make it a bit harder. One thing is certain, if I didn't write the query at all I wouldn't have a chance at a sale. And if I don't give enough facts to bring the items alive, then I've also written a letter that will reap no reward. The query as written is an attempt to walk that narrow ribbon leading to the pot of gold. The items withheld are token insurance. But most of the query, as with most queries, is done on faith. (The vast majority of publications are honorable. Probably about the same ratio as the writers selling to them.)

Last, there is no reason to mention my publishing credits, though one article in juvenile nonfiction is noted. If the letter reads well, speaks truth with authority, and offers to cite verifiable sources, that should be enough.

## Reply to the Query

A few minutes and a few stamps, two envelopes, and some paper isn't a bad gamble on earning from $25 to several hundred simply to rework some facts that weren't being overused anyway. The reply was cordial but formal: no thanks. I guess I'll just have to wait for somebody else's list book to pop up. Or sell these tidbits as fillers. No pot of gold today.

---

*"Query letters should detail the main points of the subject matter. If a proposed article of a Lions Club program is submitted, it should specify the extent of the project, how exactly the Lions are involved and how the community benefits; if a fund-raising project, how much money is raised. For general interest articles, the subject matter should be outlined clearly and the writer should determine specifically how the story's objectives will be pursued. All too often, a proposed story will cover a broad topic without indicating how, in a short magazine article, the subject can be narrowed in order to carry a definite message. The query letter should also contain a proposed word length."*

Bob Kleinfelder, Senior Editor, *The Lion* Magazine (Lions Club International)

# 6

# A Good Query Is Almost Negotiable Tender

Let's set up a hypothetical story and follow it from query to publication. The subject is Lassie.

While pursuing other research, let's say that you stumble upon the December, 1939, issue of *The Saturday Evening Post* containing the first publication of "Lassie Come-Home," by Eric Knight. You probe a bit and find out that the short story was really a book nobody would publish, so in fact Lassie was born, in a literary way, in that issue. Let's go a step further and say that it is seven months short of Lassie's fortieth or fiftieth "birthday." Your idea: to celebrate the gala event by looking back at what the world's most famous dog has been through during that period.

## Idea

You have a salable idea. What you need next is a list of potential markets plus enough support data to make the idea come alive in a query letter.

## Possible Markets

One possible market is obvious: the source of the original story, *The Saturday Evening Post*. Other types of magazines that might want to run a family-oriented, pet-based story are general interest, animal, in-flight, women's, children's, and a half-dozen more. So you draw up a list of those fields, then determine an order for querying.

# Market Study

To extend our example further, let's say that *Our Family Magazine* appears to be the best market for your idea. It pays handsomely, on acceptance, and runs reams of well written general interest-humor-nostalgia copy each month. You head to the library to read the issues for the past three months, paying particular attention to two stories dealing with related topics: a National Velvet movie remake, with a look back at the original, and an expose of Smokey the Bear, fact and fiction. You note the approaches these pieces take, their length, the amount and kind of humor used, and the way that animals are treated.

# Query Letter

Then you write a query letter to Mr. Leon Stokes, the managing editor, explaining your idea, bring it to life, include your writing background, and add suggestions about illustrations.

"Interesting facts" about Lassie are found in the library listings under movies, radio (yes, Lassie was a radio star, barking and growling over the airwaves on command), TV, and "famous animals/pets." You tell Stokes that the first Lassie in the movies was really "Pal," a male so full of thistles and burrs when he came to audition he was literally a sore sight. That collies had been avoided in American movies because they were thought to be too nervous in front of the camera. That "Pal" had been so hard to control as a puppy, his owner actually paid Rudd Weatherwax, "Lassie's" trainer, to keep him. That when the collie kissed Roddy McDowall, in "Lassie Come Home," after bounding across a schoolyard in a scene that brought tears to the eyes of a war-worn America, he was actually licking ice cream off the boy's face. That the story itself was told to Knight when he was a boy growing up in Yorkshire, England, by an uncle who claimed that it was true, and that "come-home" dogs were reputedly common in that area, trained to come home the night after they were sold, to be resold again! Finally, that Eric Knight never saw the 1943 movie. He was killed in the war before it was released.

These facts are artfully woven into the query letter for one reason: to convince Leon Stokes that his readers will find the full piece as tantalizing as the excerpts he has just read.

You write the letter, fold it, insert it into a large envelope with another, smaller, self-addressed and stamped envelope (SASE), and mail the lot to *Our Family Magazine*. Then you wait, patiently.

## "Go-ahead" Reply

Let's imagine that Stokes is delighted with the idea and sees it fitting in the coming December issue, with a cover in honor of the anniversary. But he doesn't know you or your work. He replies, tempering his enthusiasm and noting that if the piece can be in his hands within a month, he would gladly consider it "on speculation." A "go-ahead" letter!

## Dilemma

A dilemma. The research and writing will take considerable time. If he rejects the final manuscript, you'll have to redo it to fit some other magazine's needs. Should you go ahead on chance or keep querying until you get a firm guarantee of purchase before investing the time?

Be realistic. Who is going to pay you $500, or even $100, to write something for them when they don't even know if you are literate? Granted, you wrote a captivating query, but who (besides me) publishes query letters? And how does the editor really know that you wrote the query letter at all, that you wouldn't just take the cash and dash, or, even if you have the most honorable of intentions (an assumption not always cast on writers), you will be able to provide copy that is even printable?

In my own case, I look upon speculation replies, like Stokes', as money all but in hand. Since I began using queries I've sold from 85% to 90% of the pieces submitted on speculation — and the rest, with two exceptions, to other buyers.

Can you reasonably expect Stokes or any editor to wire you a purse of doubloons just because you promise him a Pulitzer Prize piece? Hardly. Would you if you were the editor? First you must submit copy as good or better than that promised in the query letter. Presume that Stokes pencilled the item on his December calendar when you were given the go-ahead. Your chances of appearing in that issue are better than 50-50 — unless you ruin them. Even if the copy isn't usable as sent, there is the possibility that he will suggest ways to improve it, so you can try again with a rewrite. (Even if the answer is no, you can still sell it to other markets on your market list.)

## Write the Reply

Therefore, if you get a go-ahead on speculation, stir that library dust, pound the keys, and whip up a first-class article. Think beyond that first sale. The next time you confront Stokes with a blue-ribbon idea in a well written query you won't be an unknown, and he just might send you that $500 in advance. Even if he doesn't (and most editors never do), each future go-ahead will be closer to a sure sale, as long as you consistently send copy that matches what you promise in your query and is as well written as the other articles in the publication.

## You're in Print!

Say that you do churn out several thousand words bringing the many Lassies back to full, tail-wagging life. Stokes likes your piece, sends a check, and about November you receive from one to five copies of the coming issue of *Our Family Magazine*. You're in print!

Sound too simple? There's no magic to selling your writing. Perhaps eight of ten sales follow that pattern. The highest hurdle comes not in selling a queried manuscript but in finding a publication willing to look at your idea. Still, if the idea has public appeal, if your queries are specifically tailored to the respective publications, if those publications sell to the readers most interested in your idea, and if your letter shows by its content and form that you are a capable writer, most ideas you set forth for print can result in a paycheck.

## ... or Rejected

Let's throw some curves into the set-up, as examples of how queries are still the best use of time and energy. Let's say that Stokes hates collies, is up to his nostrils in nostalgia, and has an odious father-in-law with your first name. For some mysterious reason he rejects your query.

Disappointing, but not fatal. Go to the next magazine on your list, read it, tailor a query to its needs, then wait again. Mrs. Lulu Potts, editor-in-chief, waxes ecstatic in her reply. "It's wonderful, I'm so excited, ... " So you conjure up a manuscript that is properly "wonderful" and send it to her. She rejects it flat! "I've changed my mind," she says, and that is that.

You have a number of responses. You can fire off a scalding reply questioning whether she has a mind to change. That will fail to get the piece bought. It may close her market to you forever.

You can kick Lassie in the penside and forget the whole thing, which also won't feed the chickens.

You can reread your copy of the query letter and see how your manuscript differs from what Lulu had been led to expect. Or see if it is so far below publishable quality that any editor would reject it, however wide-eyed he or she was at the outset. In either case you must make corrections the next time around. If the manuscript is solid but not what the query paints, change brushes and paint a truer likeness in the next query. If the manuscript is poorly done, do it the second time as you should have the first.

The reality is that you still have a manuscript in your hand. What should you do with it? You can either query about it to the next market on the list or send it with a cover letter (not mentioning that others found it unusable!) to that same market.

We've been too hard on Ms. Potts. Let's imagine that she did respond to the manuscript and was no less delighted with the final version than she was excited by your query. Except for one thing: you had spent all of your time writing about oddities, like history and fame, and she really wanted a piece about Lassie's grooming. "Will you please rewrite the article making that the main focus, with examples?"

In other words, no sale unless you invest more time in research and writing. Free time.

If you know where to find the information that she wants and the alterations would be fast and minor, grumble to yourself, do the rewrite and be sure to ask for more specific guidelines from Ms. Potts the next time before preparing another piece for her magazine.

Yet if she is really asking for a totally different manuscript, that's not nearly so bad. Set aside the gem she has rejected to sell elsewhere and write the last word on collie grooming for Lulu, accepting her check with both grace and haste. Then sell the manuscript you set aside to another editor, either through another query or by submitting the manuscript, with a cover letter, directly by mail.

There is no end to the imaginary pitfalls one can invent to confuse and frighten you. But why? Most new writers do enough of that inventing themselves. Once you find an interested buyer, if the piece lives up to the expectations you created in the query letter, it is rare that it won't be bought.

Later we will discuss simultaneous queries, reprints, second rights, and overseas sales. Those are the areas where exquisite complications most often occur.

# 7

# It Starts With an Idea . . .

You can think up the most exciting idea in the world but if others won't read past the first sentence, your idea will suffer a silent, unprinted commercial death.

The crassness of that truth disturbs many new writers often fresh from the less competitive pastures of academia, where everything written is read and matched to a grade. In the commercial world, though, nothing forces anyone to read what you write, much less pay to buy the publication it's in. And if no one will read it or buy the publication, you won't get rich by writing nonfiction. You won't even get poor.

So that is the test that must be applied to every idea before it is framed in a query: will it be bought and read if it gets in print?

The editor knows what his readers will buy, and that determines what he will buy from you.

I once researched a potential article about the circumflex in Portuguese, an odd-looking hat-like symbol ^ that occasionally appears atop the a, e, and o. This curious relic has a noble and intriguing history, first seen in Greek before changing form and use in other tongues. Still, I couldn't find more than a handful of philologists and Lusophiles who could even pronounce the word, much less want to read about it. The topic was doomed. It never got to the querying stage.

On the other hand, the Lassie story has been the object of at least 50 queries, has appeared in print twenty-plus times, and may appear as a book about how pets find their way home over long distances. The idea has a huge market: a nation of dog lovers from 6 to 60 who grew up with the tricolored collie. They remember the movies and TV series and want to read about how they and America's best known dog have aged together.

Still, it's not enough to have an idea to write a query. A thinking writer can churn out 50 ideas an hour. Most of them don't merit querying because their scope is too narrow or shallow, they have just been written about, they are outdated, or they are too dull. The ones that survive are those with some built-in appeal to a sizable portion of the reading, paying public.

# Ideas That Sell

New writers think that to sell they must have a unique, original, or singular idea. Actually, ideas that sell are usually the reverse: they concern the things that affect you and me every day. They disturb, amuse, irk, or inspire us. How will we get around when gas hits $4 a gallon? Will another Messiah appear in our lifetime, and will we recognize Him/Her? When will there be a vaccine against cancer? How can I keep going when it all seems so hopeless? Why can't kids read or write? How can I get more sex, happiness, money, love, friends, security, appreciation, joy, satisfaction — one, any, or all!

If you think of an idea annually, it may not be salable. If you think of it weekly, you may have something. If you think of it daily, zero in. (If you think of it five times a day, you have an obsession!)

# Study Your Markets

What do readers want to know about? Pick a publication in which you'd like to see your material published. Study its table of contents for the past six months. Reduce each article to the topic it discusses. Those are the subjects its readers pay to explore. Take those words and move out. Ask new questions about those topics. Focus on one that particularly interests you. Research it, query, write the manuscript, and when you see yourself on those pages wonder why it all seemed so hard before.

Don't shy away from a subject because it has been in print often. When many think of travel, they think of Hawaii, Rio de Janeiro, Hong Kong, Paris, Switzerland, Carpinteria, Ireland, or perhaps Nova Scotia. Take any of those places and see what working questions about them served as the core of articles in the *Reader's Guide to Periodical Literature* (RGPL) for the past two years. List those questions. Than ask six more. In the new six will be hiding one or many salable query ideas.

# Timing

Timing is crucial. That means getting a good topic into print before others do. To make sure that an identical idea hasn't just been printed, check the RGPL, the contents of the magazines most likely to have run the topic, major newspaper indexes, and book titles in the subject listings of your library.

There's another aspect to timing. Nothing angers an editor like a query with a dynamite idea that must be used immediately — or sooner. Remember, the query is to be written by a professional for professional consideration. Pros know that magazines have a fairly long lead time. Monthlies often need copy and illustrations three to four months in advance. Sunday supplements are often finalized six weeks or longer before publication, and even daily newspapers can take up to a week to work in copy. The moral is plain: plan ahead, way ahead.

If you are hoping to write about the Boston Marathon in April, query in August or September. Holiday issues need even more time. Query a year in advance or your idea may be held from print for two years! With your luck that editor probably pays on publication!

# 8

## ... That Fits Through an Hourglass

t helps if you can visualize where the query letter, an idea, and you are in relation to the publication. Think of an hourglass on its side. You are on one end and the publication is on the other. At the narrow passageway sits the editor.

You must take an idea and reduce it in scope to fit through the opening. Let's say that you want to write about baseball for a major sports magazine. Great! It needs stories about baseball. But the whole topic is too large to squeeze through, so you must pick a particular aspect of baseball, an angle or item or way of seeing facts that will excite readers and at least interest the editor.

You decide to focus on baseball in Brazil, especially among Japanese Brazilians living in the São Paulo area.

Now you must present your idea in a query letter that will gain approval of the editor or, even though the new topic will fit through, the editor won't let it. The bald fact is that editors can stop any idea you try to pass through the funnel. On the other hand, they need good ideas, and to survive as editors they must let enough get through to fill their pages each week or month.

The analogy may be a bit simplistic but it accurately puts our parts into a proper relationship. An even simpler, or more simplistic, example would have the editor behind a door you must go through to appear in the magazine. The door opens only when you say the right words in an acceptable way. The words are framed in the query.

# 9

# When Should You Send the Manuscript?

**W**hen you get a go-ahead from a query, the editor giving you the nod is high in your concerns. Unfortunately, you are far less important to that editor, who has a dozen articles in process plus other editorial worries, like query letter reading to find more ideas for future copy. The editor will remember your idea, maybe your name, but likely little more.

For that reason, I query only when I think I can get the manuscript to the editor within a three-week period. That way, from the date I get the green light until the "package" is en route, there is a sufficiently short period of time for the editor to have it and me in mind, and, should it require some rewrite, there is still time to make alterations before publication.

Further, I often state in the query that the manuscript and attachments will be in the editor's hands within three weeks.

There is one major exception. When travel is required I query as much as six months in advance, telling the editor when I plan to leave and return. To the return date I add about three weeks and promise to have the copy in the editor's hands by that date.

I've tried to convince the editor that I am a professional, at least by content and the appearance of my query, so that same professionalism must extend to honoring time commitments. Thus I do everything possible to get the copy in his hands within 21 days.

Yes, I have missed deadlines, but rarely. In each case, before the third week, I wrote or called the editor explaining why a delay would take place and when the copy would arrive — within 10 days, maximum, of the earlier deadline.

I've had editors tell me that they like receiving the copy so quickly. It gives them a chance to see the material while the idea is still hot. I think it results in many more sales, though there is no way to prove that. It also forces me to get to the writing quickly, and to do a more thorough pre-query job of researching and annotating sources.

---

*"We prefer receiving query letters rather than entire nonfiction pieces. Queries don't have to be logged in and can be handled more quickly than manuscripts. The editor can give the writer suggestions along with the go-ahead on the query, so the manuscript will stand a better chance of coming out the way we want it to.*

*"We want our query writers to explain why we can trust their facts: are they experts, do they have first-hand knowledge, or can they at least cite reliable references? We want to see from the query that the article will contain lively writing that will appeal to children. A lead or sample paragraph and a brief outline of the intended subject will give us a good idea of what the author has to offer.*

*"Since we have to judge the writer's abilities by the form, content, and organization of the query, grammar and spelling mistakes certainly don't help.*

*"We prefer tightly focussed queries to lists of topics. A list doesn't give enough clues about the treatment of any one subject and good ideas may be rejected because the editor has too many unanswered questions.*

*"One other thing — many of our rejections occur because authors want to write the same old subjects. If we bought all the articles we're offered on hummingbirds entitled 'Nature's Little Helicopters,' we could fill several issues a year with them!"*

Claire Miller, Managing Editor, *Ranger Rick* Magazine (National Wildlife Federation)

# 10

## Research Before Writing

A query letter saves you time. It lets you delay most of the research, the interviews, and the bulk of your writing until you have a specific readership to write for and a near-promise that your work will be published and you will be paid.

How much time should you spend researching your topic before writing a query? My answer is about as precise as Abraham Lincoln's when he was asked how long a man's legs should be: "Long enough to touch the ground."

The same holds true, figuratively, for a query. You need to research your query until it is accurate and impressive and you know that you can deliver the manuscript it promises.

Suppose that it is 1975 and a bicentennial is approaching. You could write about what was going to take place in 1976. Or about 1776, the root of the celebration. Yet you suspect that both dates will be overworked. So you pick the "first Centennial," 1876. You research the idea. To your delight, you discover that 1876 was a bumper year for interesting, ironic, and humorous events, well peopled with characters whose names are still known today. You decide that a fast, fun, tightly-woven string of happenings, names, anecdotes, and ironies will be your format. What do you do next?

# Find a Market

Find markets ripe for such fun, then focus on one, identify its readers, and pluck from your pool of materials appropriate tales, events, names, and facts to make your query sparkle, as an example of what merriment and insight readers can expect in the final copy.

# Library Research

You will need a firm understanding of what happened in 1876. That requires reliable sources at hand, like Dee Brown's zesty text about that year, a guidebook from the Centennial Exhibition in Philadelphia, access to the January 1 and July 4 editions of *The New York Times* and other newspapers, plus biographies of Twain, Custer, Grant, Edison, Eddy, Tilden, Moody, etc. From those sources (and their sources, gleaned from their footnotes and bibliographies) you must select the proper choice of items for the query and final manuscript, using the interests of your potential readers as a gauge. It would be wise to find a way to relate the "first" centennial to the bicentennial too, to show the editor why he should even be interested in looking back 100 years rather than concentrating solely on the present.

# Query

Armed with the material necessary to bring your query alive, to substantiate the claims made in it, and to justify the editor's picking 1876 instead of 1976, there is no reason to research further. Write the query, note the sources for your own use later, and go on to something else. If you receive a go-ahead, reactivate the sources, find more, organize the manuscript, write it, fill in the gaps with additional research, doublecheck the facts elsewhere, edit the opus, and send it off, keeping some form of source identification in your final rough copy to substantiate any item challenged later. Tell the editor in a cover note that you can cite the sources of all points made in the text.

# Interviewing

Interviewing is another form of research. If your piece requires comments or quotes from living sources, make certain that you can speak with them when needed. If they are readily accessible, contact them before writing the query, explaining what you have in mind and asking them a key question or two, to work their replies into the query. Should they agree to give you a longer interview later, that's all you need. Others may have to be contacted through their agents or friends. Whatever method is used, be certain they will be available and will be able to provide you with the type of information you are promising the editor.

In summary, most queries require some research. Do as much as you need to write an accurate, exciting query. Then read closely what you have written to make certain you can provide proof of every point made or implied and that you will be able to add the necessary facts, quotes, and other items promised in the query. When that is done, so are you, until you are told to send the manuscript.

---

*"A go-ahead can take place at the first reading if the writer is a substantial authority with an original idea. If either is lacking, it may take a while."*

John Fink, Editor, *Chicago* Magazine

# 11

## Then Write To The Editor as You Would Write to a Human Being

**W**hat is an editor? It's human, probably male, 35-55, harried, hairless, something like an underpaid neighbor. He's cynical, his eyes burn, and the day you write him will be the day his half-spaced kid tried to drive a 1967 Dodge through a tree. Oh yes, he's also the person you must convince, in a one-page letter, that you should be paid to write for his publication.

Lately, he's as likely to be a she, with all the above and more hair.

In either case, not only has the editor never met you, but probably never will, nor want to unless you and your prose bring the publication more readers.

If editors loved their mail and cherished the moments when they could close their doors, read leisurely, chuckle appropriately, and ponder often, that would be one thing. But most editors treat their mail as if it's radioactive, postponing its painful perusal until the next Ice Age, or at least until Thursday, late.

What depresses them is the quality of the letters and the impossibility of using all of the good ideas the better ones contain. Imagine having to choose from 100-2000 queries a month the best six or sixteen that will see print. Rejecting so many ideas would be far worse if so many of the letter writers didn't eliminate themselves by writing abysmally or saying nothing worth consideration.

To write one of those chosen articles your query must shine like a gem in a bed of pebbles.

# Read This Twice

*To make your letter shine it must convince the editor that your idea — and the treatment you are going to give it — is so special, so interesting, so vital to readers that it would be foolish not to respond at once urging that your manuscript be sent AIR MAIL SPECIAL DELIVERY.*

Remember those words. They are the heart of selling and querying. If the subject of your query isn't so special, so interesting, so vital, it will probably earn a rejection. Yet if you simply say that it is, in so many words, you've also failed to do what a selling writer must: convey those verities by the tone and content of the query itself.

If your letter doesn't make the editor want to know what's in the second paragraph because of what you said in the first, it won't work. If that editor has any doubts about the idea you are selling, the letter isn't clear. If the editor doesn't respond quickly, or at least set it aside to act upon later (or send it to others on the staff for their thoughts), you've wasted your energy. The way to keep your letter out of the rejection pile is to present a salable topic factually, excitingly, and articulately.

Having said that, every selling writer can cite a query that missed on almost every point but still resulted in a sale.

Ignore those exceptions in the beginning. Stick with money-making eye-openers that will stand out in the editor's mind. Not only do you want the editor to set your letter aside, you want that arbiter to picture the final manuscript in print, with illustrations, then write the topic on the calendar for use in a particular future issue. When the editor replies, giving you a go-ahead and perhaps suggesting a length, deadline, and amount to be paid upon acceptance, you want that editor to be waiting for the finished product with the same eager anticipation with which you waited for your reply.

The ideal query letter should convey the feeling that you and the editor are in a joint venture to delight the readers of the publication so they will show your article to their friends, who will immediately send for subscriptions so they don't miss your next appearance on those pages.

# You Are Your Query Letter

Remember, all the editor knows about you is what can be read on one page of paper, in your letter. If the letter is written on spotted butcher paper, what does that say? If it contains three misspelled (sic) words in the first paragraph, does it show a solid command of written English? If the query is duller than wet cotton yet promises an exciting article, which should be believed, the promise or the proof?

Alas, editors are about as human as we are, and they like others to succeed, especially when that success adds to their own. Give them something that will help them produce better magazines and all will prosper. Gain their confidence with solid query letters, then make good on the gain with copy as good or better than that promised. That's a formula certain to tame and win any editor.

---

*"The query should include a specific proposal, the author's qualifications, the sales message, an indication of at least some research, and an indication of how much cooperation can be expected from sources."*

John Fink, Editor, *Chicago* Magazine

# 12

## To Which Editor Should You Write?

The best way to find out to whom the query letter should be sent is to check the current *Writer's Market*. If it says "send all queries to Mr. J. Johnson, Managing Editor," the only remaining question is whether he still holds the same position. Check the most recent issue of the publication, then send your query to Johnson or the current managing editor.

If the *Writer's Market* listing doesn't indicate a person or position, try the managing editor or the section editor where your idea would most likely appear. The larger the publication, the less likely you should be writing directly to the editor-in-chief, or equivalent. More often, the managing editor or section editor weeds through queries, pulls the most promising, works them into idea possibilities for coming issues, and takes those work-ups to the editor-in-chief for discussion and/or approval, replying to you after a decision has been made.

If the publication doesn't appear in the *Writer's Market*, it means either that it has folded (and definitely isn't the place to query) or, simply, it isn't listed. Check first to see if it is still sold on a regular basis, and if so, find the list of editors (usually near the table of contents), the address, and other related information.

# Query a Current Editor

Is it really that important that you send your query to a current editor? Consider a talk I had with the managing editor of a sports magazine that had refilled his position three times in 30 months. He had a rule-of-thumb in replying to queries or manuscripts that he felt was typical, in principle, of other editors he knew. If queries or manuscripts were addressed to the first editor, gone more than two years, they were kept in a box for some weeks, unopened, and were then switched into their own SASE's, a rejection note was inserted, and the material was returned, unread. No SASE, it was dumped.

If the previous editor's name was used, since that person had departed only six months back, the queries were read as they arrived, but the manuscripts — which the magazine did not want without a previous query — were returned, unread, in about two weeks.

Any query sent to the current editor was read the day it arrived and acted upon promptly. His logic was simple: If the person hadn't read the publication for two years, which was implied by the use of the first editor's name, the writer had no idea of the substantial changes the magazine had undergone. Even the use of the previous editor's name indicated that the writer was violating a common sense requirement for professionals, that they keep current on the publications and their top staff. Using the wrong name meant that it had been at least six months since the writer had checked the publication. Even if he had flipped through a more recent copy he hadn't had enough sense to see who was the current editor to whom he should be writing!

# ... by the Right Name

Calling the editor by the wrong name isn't the brightest way to win favor. Petty? Perhaps, but the editors hold all the chips.

# 13

# When You Don't Need Query or Cover Letters

One basic question should be asked of each item at the outset: "Should it be queried before it is written?"

From that comes four follow-up questions about how that item should be sent to the editor:

(1.)    Should it be submitted, after being queried and receiving a go-ahead, without an accompanying cover letter?
(2.)    Should it be submitted, after being queried and receiving a go-ahead, with an accompanying cover letter?
(3.)    Should it be submitted without a query but with a cover letter?
(4.)    Should it be submitted without either a query or a cover letter?

Let's address ourselves to the basic question plus (1.) and (4.) here, leaving those elements involving the use of cover letters until later.

What should be queried? Nonfiction articles. Plus humorous articles (where the topic is queried and the humor is the style of the writing, not the sole purpose of the piece) and nonfiction books, soon to be explained. Syndicated and overseas items fall into the gray area where either queries or cover letters can be most appropriate, so they too will receive special discussion later.

There is no reason to send an accompanying cover letter with any of these queried items if the copy and support material (photos, captions, diagrams, etc.) are sent promptly or when promised, unless there is something new or additional the editor must know. More on that under "cover letters."

When should material be sent directly in, without a query or a cover letter?

# Greeting Cards

By the time you wrote a query, you could have typed most of the studio lines, mottoes, plaque sayings, or whatever it is you wanted to sell. And what would you say anyway? "Do you want to buy some funny greeting card lines?" Of course they do, that's why they're in the business. But how does anyone know that yours are funny, and usable, without seeing them? The same goes for card poetry, slogans, buttons, and almost anything else these publishers buy, with the exception of book or booklet ideas and new product formats, where a query should accompany an example of what you have in mind.

# Fillers

These work as an unit and are, as the name implies, copy used to fill extra space, often "ad holes." Most are 1,000 words or less, some as short as a joke or quip. For the editor to see whether the item works, if it holds together and provides the type of message needed to fill a space, the editor must see the item complete and finished. Many fillers rely upon humor, which makes them doubly important to be sent directly, to see if they are funny. (Incidentally, you can submit more that one filler at the same time. Each, of course, must be a complete and different unit.) If some special commentary is needed, that would be sent in a cover letter with the copy.

# Humor

How can you convince an editor that a humor piece is funny in a query letter? The query may have him gasping for air between guffaws but the actual piece could be flatter than the deadest Neanderthal. So save your stamps and typing finger and just send the copy itself. One thing more: a humor piece relies almost solely on its humor to be bought, like the zanies in *Mad Magazine*. If you are writing a regular article from a humorous slant, where the information is more important that the humor, call it "humorous" and query as you would with a general interest item. Again, only if additional information must be shared with the editor, which would enhance the item's sale, should you send a cover letter with the text.

# Fiction

Where the editor can't tell if the humor is funny enough through a query letter, even less can he or she tell whether the components of good fiction — characters, plot, dialog, setting, etc. — work together just because you swear, on your Mama's reputation, that they do. Let the editor read the fiction. For short stories, send in the entire work. For novels, see what the publisher has said in *Writer's Market* about how material should be submitted, then send a synopsis and key chapters or the whole manuscript, as indicated. Your mother will thank you.

---

The following topics will be discussed later in the chapters about cover letters: simultaneous submissions, reprints, direct submissions (including fillers and fiction), photos/illustrations, syndication, overseas sales, and delayed submissions.

---

*"I hate queries that show the author's never studied the magazine's content."*

John Fink, Editor, *Chicago* Magazine

# 14

# What a Good Query Looks Like

**A** query letter is a business letter, not a chatty, informal "how's-the-family" exchange between old friends, even if the editor, by chance, also happens to be an old friend. You are asking for money in exchange for a service. You want to be paid for researching, writing, and permitting the use of your labors.

So the appropriate form for such a transaction is that of a business letter: concise, direct, functional. The examples in this book show one form of business letter. For variations, consult your library for books describing and showing other forms.

Query letters should be single-spaced so they read faster and the message can be contained, if possible, on one page. They should be neat, error-free (the use of correction fluid or filler is acceptable, if the final result is easy to read), and written on white paper, unless one consistently uses a very light gray, cream, or pastel. Flaming red, white, and blue paper or white type on black paper, for example, shout "showboat" and create doubt in the editor's mind about your seriousness, maturity, or perhaps even sanity.

Put in another light, if you ran an ad asking for all qualified writers interested in preparing your biography to appear at a certain address at a stated time, and three showed up, without knowing more than you could see (like an editor with a query letter in hand), would you most likely hire: (1) a person neat in appearance, clean, and dressed in conventional form, (2) a person with a dash of mud artlessly scattered about his face and clothing, with a tear in one shoe and a price tag hanging from one sleeve, or (3) a person wearing a three-foot-tall hat with pigeon feathers poking from it, a blazing violet neck wrap that partially obscured his face and most of his torso, and electric yellow-blue high-heeled shoes?

A conventional business letter is analogous to (1). In form, not too exciting, but not too alarming either. No distractions delay or obstruct consideration of the writer's message. The second person might be like an error-filled, slapdash letter. If its writer thinks so little of the letter's appearance, can he be trusted to do a thorough job researching an article? Will the final manuscript show adherence to accuracy? Maybe, but the editor has to overcome serious misgivings created by the letter's first impression.

The third letter is akin to the third person: a screaming missive on scarlet paper typed with green ribbon, smelling of perfume (or is it rum?), and spiced with such starred and underlined "grabbers" as REPLY INSTANTLY, CHANCE-OF-A-LIFETIME, I'M YOUR PERSON, etc. It shouts so many hair-raising messages that an editor, whose reputation and scalp depend upon the writer's output, couldn't help but have grave doubts.

The point is simple: let the body of the letter sell both your idea and you as the person who should prepare it. The form of the letter should be so secondary, and supportive, that nothing delays the reader from leaping into the written message. Neither errors nor strike-overs, hand-scribbled footnotes, eye-yanking arrows, gaudy paper, or off-color ribbons should pull the reader's attention from the letter's crucial contents. Everything in the letter, stated and implied, should work in your favor. Its form should say that you are a person who is serious about writing, attentive to detail, careful, businesslike, mature, and can write well.

The editor, in most cases, has no idea who you are, if you are 9 or 90, sowing your oats or going to seed, fat or flat, Ivy League or Bush League, active or radioactive. And he or she probably doesn't care. What is wanted is a professional writer who will produce copy that will sell more copies of that editor's publication, that is accurate, well written, and submitted before or when it is due. Your letter must reinforce your image of professionalism.

All the editor knows about you at the first contact is what can be seen and read in the query letter. That is the sum total of the clues the editor must decipher in deciding whether to give you a go-ahead. If the written message of that query is extraordinarily convincing, detracting visuals in the letter's form and appearance may be overlooked. But if there are enough clues that the writer isn't professional, at least in intent, doubts will rise. Too many doubts and the query will end up in the reject pile, even though the idea posed may be very good.

---

*"I don't like to be disappointed, and I don't like to disappoint free-lance writers. If a writer tailors an article for Michiana Magazine and sends it to me unsolicited and it turns out I can't use it, he or she is disappointed. If the writer had queried me first, chances are I could have saved the writer a lot of work and postage. Sometimes the writer has no way of knowing whether the subject is appropriate for Michiana without querying. Maybe someone else already is writing on that same subject. Maybe the subject has already been covered in another part of The South Bend Tribune. Maybe I like the subject but not the way the writer has approached it.*

*"If a query is sloppily written or too sketchy or full of misspellings, I tend to think the manuscript will reflect a lackadaisical approach.*

*"But if the writer has an appealing topic and shows me in a query how to explore it interestingly with tightly written, power-packed language, I stand little chance of being disappointed when I read the manuscript.*

*"I like a query to outline the article, tell me about how many words the writer intends to supply, how soon the manuscript could be expected and what illustrative material, if any, is available."*

Bill Sonneborn, Editor, *Michiana* Magazine, of *The South Bend Tribune*

# 15

# What a Query Letter Doesn't Say

**A** query letter should be positive. Tell the editor the idea you wish to develop, what tools and special skills you bring to the task, information about your past writing experience, and so on. The rest remains unsaid. It's hard enough to sell an idea in a good query letter without saying too much and creating doubt.

## Previous Publications

For example, do you mention that you've never, or seldom, been in print before? Do you attempt to overwhelm the editor with your honesty and frankness, hoping to woo that lucky soul into giving you your first big break by laying your record bare? I wouldn't. Nor would I lie and invent publications or an impressive number of items supposedly sold. I wouldn't say a word. Rather, I'd let a tight, fast, professional-sounding query letter say it all by implication: this idea is from a writer able and eager to produce good copy needed by your publication (whether or not that writer has sold before). Don't mention previous publications unless impressive. Write so well that the editor is thinking about how to get you to write for the magazine again and again. Think big by making this query special.

# Name Change

If you're a lass and want to write for a male magazine, or the reverse, a lad for the ladies' pages, just go to it, but consider using only your initials instead of your name. Appear as B.R. Hawkins in a hockey story for *Boys Will Be Boys*, rather than as Bobbie Rae. Unless the sex switch is important to the piece — "I Was the First Lady Boxer in Latvia" — I'd write the query, give initials or a name in keeping with the topic, produce first-class copy, and cash the check.

# Money

Do you ask about money in the query? If you've been writing for a while, you will gain a feel for this kind of thing and will know your steady buyers and their ways, as well as their pay ranges. But newcomers are best advised to keep cash out of the query. Save that for later, if necessary — at least until the editor responds with a go-ahead. Frequently in the response the editor indicates an amount, plus information about length, deadline, and sometimes slant.

If your costs are going to be greater than the payment, you have two choices: adjust the costs or haggle, lovingly, to get the publication to help with or totally pay your expenses. Most magazines won't pay travel for new writers, and many won't pay expenses of any kind of speculation (not assigned) go-aheads. (Or use the material in other ways in other articles.) Just save the haggling until after you have a positive reply, where the editor is at least committed to looking at the copy with intent to use it.

*Writer's Market* lists payment rates so you should have at least an idea at the outset about the amount you can expect. First-time purchases generally stick close to the listed rates; a modest increase can be expected in later purchases.

# Knowledge of the Subject

If you have an uplifting desire to write a piece about ballooning and sail off a query on the subject, don't confide in the editor that "you know nothing about ballooning but will learn through research." If the editor's lukewarm about the subject anyway, that interest will float away. Or if the subject strikes the editor's fancy, you'll be passed over for somebody better informed. Your obligation is to learn about the topic before querying so that the slant suggested and the support material mentioned will be accurate, and the article proposed can be written. Then if you get a go-ahead and you learn about ballooning while completing your research, that is your business. The editor's interest is in a solid, reliable article about ballooning, not how and when your knowledge was gained.

Writers needn't be experts on every subject they cover. Yet to query with no knowledge and to expect an editor to pay you to learn the basic facts later is to underestimate the seriousness of professional writing.

Study the subject well before firing off your query, because if you don't, the time will come when you will be unable to find 200 words to back up the best made promise of 2000, and that will cost you an article and a client. Forty-five minutes in a library or talking with an expert will save you much time and shame.

Which backs us into another thing left unsaid in a query: a promise for an article that nobody can write.

# Unwritable Topics

No sane editor (which includes most) would believe that the Empire State Building is made of snow or that Superman really lived. Yet there is a huge playfield between what everybody knows and what nobody will believe, and free-lancers often find themselves skirting its edges.

If you propose writing an article proving that popcorn causes sterility, you had better have scientifically acceptable proof and sterile examples before you even think about a query. If you want to prove that dogs find their way home over long distances by reading maps, the same thing applies. You'd better have a kennel of dogs, or at least a few, who can take a roadmap and find a freeway intersection, plus explanations of how this alarming ability works, before you dust off your typewriter and start twisting the editor's tail.

The key word here is substantiation. Without it, that playfield can turn into a graveyard for aspiring but unprepared beginners.

---

*"I find it difficult to over-estimate the importance of query letters, especially as it concerns a specialized magazine such as (The Lion) . . . The necessity for sending a query letter, whether it be for a proposed article of general interest or for one reporting on a Lions Club project, should be obvious. Surprisingly, I get scores of manuscripts each year not even remotely relative to the editorial needs of our magazine. Why a writer would waste the time, effort and postage in submitting a full-length manuscript, perhaps even with photos (in focus or not), without first determining if we could use it is beyond me.*

*"By all means, send a query. Our guidelines specify the type of general interest we can use. Even if a freelancer 'knows' we can use a story he's come upon of a Lions Club project, a query letter would still be advisable. We may have already featured the activity in the magazine or I may have specific details I want included in the story. Unless the writer is very lucky, the chances of scoring on a first try without a query first are definitely a long-shot."*

Bob Kleinfelder, Senior Editor, *The Lion* Magazine (Lions Club International)

# 16

# What You Can Expect Back When

**E**very good query deserves a response. The question is what kind of response and when

Market listings usually indicate response times, which generally vary from a week to many months. Those times refer to manuscripts. Queries, from my experience, are answered sooner, within a week to ten days on an average. Even when an editor dallies, the delay is seldom as long as that indicated in the *Writer's Market*.

The type of response you can expect is very much related to the type and quality of query letter sent. A well written, thorough, exciting query almost always gets a personal reply from an editor, whether that editor is interested or not. Even rejections to such queries often include an invitation to query again. That is logical, since a well done query tells an editor that this is a professional writer who may later have something valuable to offer.

## Rejections

To a good query an editor will often say why the idea can't be considered at present: a similar piece is in hand or en route, it is too close to something recently used, the idea sits too far to the side of the readers' interests, the setting is outside the publication's main circulation, etc. The editor might suggest a different angle or slant, or that a history piece be set in a different time frame. The reward of a good query letter is that the editor is aware of you for future purchases. (I normally follow a warm reply to a query, though a rejection, with another query on a different subject fairly soon, while my name is fresh. In the second query, I mention the topic of the first, in case it's the topic and not my name the editor recalls.)

Having said that, a mimeographed rejection to your query doesn't necessarily imply that the query was poorly written. Some editors simply do not send personal notes. You will learn who they are, though hopefully your other queries will generate so much work that rejections in general will diminish and the impersonal denials will become sad memories of an early writing past.

Unfortunately, even poor queries sometimes draw personal replies, usually negative in result though harmless enough in tone. So a personal response isn't a reliable gauge as to the worth of a query. It says something, however. If you receive nothing but an unbroken string of faded, general rejections, take a hard look at what your queries are saying, how they are saying it, what they look like, and where they are being sent. Then ask yourself if the ideas you are trying to market aren't so limited in interest that there are too few readers to justify their being used.

Another thought about rejections is so obvious that I would exclude it if I hadn't seen it so frequently violated: if an editor says no, don't try the same query with a different editor at the same publication. Good ideas are often discussed at regularly scheduled meetings of the general editorial staff. If your idea reached that level, then was rejected, the second editor would naturally follow suit. Even worse, there is usually just one editor who handles the type of manuscript you propose, so if you've already addressed that editor the first time, then tried another, the second submission will likely filter back to the first editor on the second attempt! In short, the only way to sell that publication would be for the first editor to expire, flee, or retire, and it seems to be a rule in granite that any editor who rejects a query will never do any of the three, while editors who accept queries have the permanence of vapors.

# Standard Rejections

The form that standard rejections take is usually the blandest possible. "Sorry, this does not meet our present editorial needs. Thank you for considering us. Good luck in placing it elsewhere." Or something similar. Paltry stuff for your investment of time, brain power, postage, research, and hope. Still, it's better than writing the entire manuscript, then receiving the same unkind message.

# Rejections With Teeth

If you get a rejection with teeth, you probably earned it. I recall one from my own Dark Ages that says it all. I had tried to hawk a humor short about motion sickness to an in-flight magazine. Not a surplus of brightness there. (Because it was humor and a short, I sent the manuscript directly, without a query.) Imagine a passenger just settling back after a roller coaster take-off, nausea bag in one hand, magazine in the other, launching into a laugh-filled ditty about the galling horrors of air sickness! I forget the editor's exact words. Some weren't in my writing vocabulary. Something about my ability to type in a straight jacket, with the assurance that his in-flight competition was the perfect place for such a revolting topic. Similar language can be expected when you try to pawn pornography to church journals, abortion studies to *Jack and Jill*, and life-after-death pieces to retirement monthlies.

# "Go-aheads"

The "go-aheads" are much more fun to read. "Let's see what you have ... " is a common reply, scribbled in fourth-grade Palmer at the bottom of a query. Or "send me the article on speculation." Never "this is the best query I've ever read. How can the manuscript be anything but better? $3000 enclosed. Rush copy — we are holding the next issue. How can we ever thank you for picking us?"

Actually, positive replies are often as bland as the rejections — with reason. You query about a new baseball bat being proposed for *Slugger Magazine*. The editor, Bob Lester, reads your letter. He likes the idea and is enthused by the query. He thinks you can send accurate, well written copy soon. But Bob doesn't know you. He doesn't want to promise too much in case the manuscript is unusable. He wants to encourage you to finish your research and write the text for his publication, but he doesn't want to risk cash on the outcome. He tells you to go ahead and he'll look at the result. No promise to pay. He has a thousand reasons why. Factors beyond his control. The magazine may fold. He may be flooded by better copy from his regular suppliers. The topic may appear in a competitive journal. His stockpile is filled. And so on.

The result is a bland go-ahead, with the true conditions unstated and hopefully not too obvious. You do the research and writing at your own expense, and if it meets his needs when he reads it, or later, he will make a commitment.

# Legalities

There's another problem too. If an editor says "yes, send me your article about ratfish (or whatever), I'll pay $500 for it," that editor has sealed a contract. The three elements of contract — offer, acceptance, and consideration — have been met. And if you send in the worst job imaginable, but about ratfish and on time, you are due $500.

Mind you, getting the $500 may be a task, but legally you are in the right. The editor made no stipulation about quality or acceptance contingent upon approval of the text.

That hasn't gone unnoticed by editors: their first words to their replacements are "Don't say YES!" Especially when they can say, "let me see it," and get you to do the work at no risk, then make a decision when the product is in hand. Unfair? Fairness is an issue. But beginners trying to break into print and establish themselves as reliable word-smiths who can produce for publication must accept the reality. Fairness here is for academics and lawyers, sadly. Bland go-aheads from queries, on speculation, are the reality for newcomers.

## Paying on Publication

Those editors who pay on publication take it many steps further: they will pay, maybe, at some undefined time in the future if the publication still exists and the present editor is still around and something better hasn't come along to bounce the piece out of the pile, or until the facts are dated and the topic out of favor. Which is why I never query a publication-payer, except with rewrites or reprints, where the main piece has already sold and the time involvement on my part is slight. Then, if it's used, it's all profit.

## Abnormal Replies

If you write a good query, gird yourself for two kinds of replies: bland personal rejections, with an invitation to query again soon, or a fairly low key go-ahead, on spec. Anything else and I pay particular attention.

A printed rejection sets me to seeing what went wrong in my query and attempting to correct it the next time out.

A hearty acceptance that leaps beyond the bounds of blandness puts me to work quickly, to get the best possible manuscript in that editor's hands, before he sobers up or the publisher catches on.

Any form of acceptance or go-ahead will result in more correspondence, of course. You must write a manuscript that lives up to the query's promises, altered to meet any suggestions by the editor in his go-ahead reply. The manuscript and supporting data (maps, photos, charts, etc.) should be sent by the time indicated.

# Manuscript Submission Replies

The editor's second letter, announcing the fate of your submission, can take far longer than the query response. I figure a month at the second step, often longer. Sometimes the editor will acknowledge receipt of the manuscript. More often it is assumed that you know the procedure: the "package" you sent must be read by your editor, and often the editor's editor; the illustrations must be reviewed by the art or graphics editor, and so on. At the very least, the manuscript and attachments will be discussed again by the group at its regular meeting. The process takes time. Anxious time for you. Time to send other queries to other publications about other ideas.

Even then, after all the wait, the reply can be negative. At that point, though, you have a right to expect a personal note rather than a printed rejection without comments. (If I received the latter, I'd write and ask why the material wasn't used. I'd also cross the publication off my list for future queries — for a year, at least.)

At times the manuscript will be rejected but the editor will suggest ways that it might be altered to be made usable. I'd act on those suggestions and do the rewrite as indicated, to save the time I had already invested in research and writing the original manuscript.

If the manuscript is rejected with a personal note, the reasons may sound limp: "no longer as vital a topic as before," "reduction of copy space," etc. The editor may be letting you down softly. The manuscript may not be nearly so good as your query led the editor to expect. It lacks the vigor of the query, it has too little factual substance, you took a different slant or changed the conclusions. . . . The editor doesn't want to discourage you totally, but the copy can't be used as is. Worse yet, the editor doesn't think you can bring it up to an acceptable level. The rewriting, the time, the letters, all take too much investment for too little certainty of yield. You blew it.

What do you do next? Query another publication, this time matching your promise to what you have in hand to offer. Or send the actual manuscript to another publication, with a cover letter, as is or rewritten for the new readership, leaving unmentioned that it was already rejected elsewhere. Put the first editor on hold for a while, to let the sour taste leave both of your mouths, before querying that editor again. Don't mention the first manuscript in the subsequent query. Start fresh. Just don't forget that hard-learned lesson: the manuscript you send the editor must always be as good as the one you promised in a good query!

---

*"For a free-lance writer who has not yet been published in* Meetings and Conventions, *the query letter can be critical. Spelling and grammar should be impeccable. The letter should be typed, not hand-written. It should show that the writer has some familiarity with our magazine and audience. He or she should concentrate on one or two ideas, with a paragraph of elaboration.*

*"Clips of previously published material can be very helpful, especially if the subject matter is not too far from what we use.*

*"It's a good idea to say at the end of your letter, 'I'll call in 10 days to get your reaction.' This pushes me to read the letter, even if I'm busy.*

*"For the writer whose work I've used, the query should simply state the idea(s), the rationale for it and how the writer intends to deal with the subject.*

*"I like an SASE with the letter. It makes life easier."*

*"I prefer letters to phone calls. I'm often too busy to really pay attention to a call and am likely to say, send an outline, simply to get the writer out of my hair.*

*"I prefer a single-page query letter to a long one, but I have read long ones if the idea seemed good.*

*"The more professional the writer sounds the better. I don't like 'I would love to write for your magazine,' or 'I read a recent issue, and it seemed terrific,' or 'I'm dying to be published.' We're a business publication and a query letter should be business-like."*

Mel Hosansky, Editor-in-Chief, *Meetings & Conventions*

# 17

## Should You Send Queries Simultaneously to Different Editors?

There is only one limitation to the number of different queries about topics you should send out simultaneously or concurrently, and that is the number of pieces you can write should each editor say yes.

Naturally you wouldn't send a query unless you wanted to write the item queried about, so each letter must be your best effort to interest, then sell, an editor.

Still, nobody succeeds with each letter, and it is a bit absurd to assume that you are the exception. There are too many unknowns: what the editor has given go-ahead's to from others' queries or is already in type for the next or coming issues, what that editor abhors and will never use, what the competition favors and the editor avoids, and so on. So there will be rejections of the best written queries.

## Different Queries

I try to keep at least 10 queries alive at a time, knowing that about a third will bring first-response go-aheads. About a third of the queries sent will be rejected outright, usually with a note saying why; the other third will fall into the delayed category, requiring follow-up correspondence, occasionally no reply, sometimes a change in focus and a later sale. When I see my writing load backing up, I limit queries to those higher priced markets I have sold to before.

# Same Queries to Different Editors

The usual question, though, doesn't refer to that situation, which is easy to comprehend. It refers to the number of the same queries a writer can send simultaneously to different editors. Which is harder to answer.

Again, a query is, in legal terms, an offer to sell a specific item to a publisher. You can sell an item as often as you wish. The problem comes when a potential purchaser wants to buy it with some degree of exclusivity. If that purchaser wants to buy "all rights," it can be sold only once. If "first rights" are the buyer's wish, it can only be sold after it has appeared in print on that editor's pages. In either case you cannot initially sell the same rights simultaneously to different publications.

That's fine, you reply, but I know that if I query five times I'll be lucky to get one nibble, much less two bites, or sales, so what's wrong with shortening my odds and speeding up the process?

That's why the question is a hard one to answer. What you are asking is done, mostly by low-selling beginners.

It is risky — and skirts too close to being unethical. Say that you do find the golden egg and have three hungry editors panting after the same gilded shell. To query and sell either to more than one editor or the highest bidder, you may have to wriggle out of two potential sales, pretending their replies never arrived, in the hope that the third will in fact buy your manuscript at a stated or presumed rate; or write two or three pieces so similar that none of the editors, if they find out, will hire you again; or another of a half-dozen such profitless, amateurish games.

Worse yet, hard as it is to imagine, editors have friends. Other editors may be old college colleagues or next-door neighbors, or their staffs may talk to each other. When each becomes aware that you have queried the other about the same topic, hard feelings — or at least some tough questions — may well result.

# Fine in Specific Markets

In some areas there is no difficulty. Newspapers, with the exception of national distributors, limit their rights to the area in which they are circulated. Thus you could query newspapers in Chicago, Atlanta, and Boston at the same time, and sell to each. But not to both Chicago papers or areas where they overlap, like South Bend and Milwaukee.

Another writing field with limited circulation is the in-flights, which serve a distinct segment of the country or world and usually do not object to the same piece being sold to other in-flights in non-overlapping areas. Regional and religious magazines also have limited distribution and can be queried in the same way.

# Difficulty is with Exclusivity

But when it comes to sending the same query letter to two or three national publications that purchase some degree of exclusivity, it is foolish to run such a risk. There are other, better ways of getting additional income yardage from the same idea.

Let me share an actual example, which is amplified in the sample query section in Part Six.

In the late 1970's, while writing for major magazines about running, I became particularly interested in women in the post-50 category as their times came tumbling down. Three of the world's fastest women runners in that age group then lived in California. A sub-three-hour marathon is a true accomplishment for any person, but the thought that a female quinquagenarian might cover 26.2 miles in that time seemed an impossibility — until the times of these top contenders began slipping closer and closer.

How could I approach a number of magazines simultaneously with an article about this feat? One way would be to send the same query to all of the magazines. A better, more professional way would be to look deeper into the topic and see how the same material might be worked from three or more different angles, then query editors from those points of approach.

Possible slants might be: (1) a short biography of each of the three athletes, (2) a longer piece featuring all three and discussing their running a possible sub-three-hour marathon, or (3) an article discussing running in the post-50 set, using these gals and perhaps male counterparts as examples of graying excellence in racing flats.

Who would be interested in a biography of such a runner? For starters, a running magazine, so that's where I concentrated. The May, 1979, issue of *The Runner* contains the result, a 1000-word short, with photo, about Margaret Miller. (The piece was later published in a book by the same group. They queried me asking for permission to reuse it and pay me again!)

All three women were from California, so I sought another magazine with a California readership. In the March, 1979, issue of *Air California Magazine* appeared an article about Miller, Carol Cartwright, and Ruth Anderson, with photos by my colleagues Skip Matheson and Steve Koletty.

I queried the retirement magazines about the "graying marathoners" but was too late: they were up to their singlets in old jogging stories.

These are three obvious approaches to this topic. At least ten more could have been built around this trio.

The point should be obvious. Almost any theme can be expanded into a series of related yet different articles for different markets, each worthy of its own querying campaign, each query sent for the purpose of achieving its own sale.

---

*"The query should exhibit the author's ability to write a solid piece well."*

John Fink, Editor, *Chicago* Magazine

# 18

## Should You Query by Phone?

A few publications in the *Writer's Market* prefer telephone queries, while many more list a number with their addresses. Yet there's only one time when I'd initiate my contact with a publication by phone that didn't specifically request it: if I had an item so hot it had to be used almost immediately.

Having said that, I once did use the telephone and wound up with nearly $1500 in speculation go-aheads which, with one exception, turned into paid articles. I joined a gold hunting expedition to the Oriente section of Ecuador on the headwaters of the Amazon (actually the tributaries of the Napo River), and in the long shot that we didn't find gold and I survived, I wanted to back up my investment with offsetting articles. The group was leaving in ten days!

So I called a men's fraternal magazine and got story leads in Colombia and Ecuador. A travel magazine wanted an item about Bogota, and a consortium of three religious magazines went together on a piece about missionary work in Ecuador in which each church was taking part.

A camping journal wondered about backpacking in the foothills of the Andes. I simply told each that I was headed that way, spoke Spanish like a native (in an area where most of the "natives" knew only Indian tongues!) and could handle my own photography. They provided the subjects, letters of introduction, and bountiful good will. The church group even advanced $100 — a true and unrequested act of faith. Friends called it a miracle.

There was a hook, though. Each publication was located in the greater Chicago area where I then lived, and I had time to visit most of the editors in person, after the phone contact, to sound out the specifics about what they wanted in the overseas report. In all, quite the reverse of most query approaches.

## Contact Too Superficial

Why I counsel against a telephone query, except in rare and special situations like the one just cited, is that the contact is too superficial and may be as easily forgotten as the go-ahead may have been given. I like to have a well written letter on the editor's desk to be read at leisure and thought about before replying. Even though the first letter may miss the target, good query letters are in themselves impressive. A quick phone call lacks that lasting impact.

## Why the Rush?

Few topics are so urgent that they require a quick reply. In fact, editors, being like me, probably resent being asked to respond immediately to a question that should be given thought.

## Degrees of Seriousness

I take a go-ahead reply quite seriously, and find that if my query letter has been thorough and professional, editors respond in the same frame of mind. I know from talking with them that they usually jot the topic and your name on the calendar in the month when your finished manuscript might be used. Phone queries don't get pencilled in until you are known, usually through past items in their publications. And those past items usually began with written queries.

# Advantages of Distance

A minor thought should perhaps be added. There is a certain formality and safe distance to a query letter that has its virtues. Some people simply don't communicate well by phone. They may stammer or beat around the bush, they may be intimidated by the editor's name or position, they may have a voice that grates or dances over the octaves. Or they may be the type who think before writing but don't before speaking, or think so slowly or fully they sound simpleminded to those who don't know them.

Your purpose is to draw the editor's attention to an idea you want to write for his or her publication. A phone conversation may well distract from that purpose, where a well written letter wouldn't. Why take the chance unless you must? When you know the editor, or the editor initiates the call, these factors become far less important.

---

*"One well developed query is probably worth more than a long list, but sometimes a list is useful as a check-off for indicating interest in subject matter."*

John Fink, Editor, *Chicago* Magazine

# 19

## Should You Query in Person?

Fortunately, this is impossible in most cases. The editor works in New York City or Chicago and you live in Seattle or Ginger Flats.

Even if you live down the street from the top dog, I'd resist the temptation to cut short the business approach until you have established a good working relationship. Even then I'd take special care to keep my writing contacts clearly that.

## Sell Your Writing

The reason is simple enough: you have a product to sell, your writing. That has little to do with your personality, good looks, or boundless charm. The editor doesn't need to like you to print your works. The chemistry takes place on the page, and the personalities between the idea and print are of little importance.

So why put your person in the way of your prose? The idea you want to sell must first catch the editor's interest, and your treatment of that topic is what matters. The editor is busy; you are eager to sell. If you pop into the office with an idea half-formed, or even fully-formed and the editor isn't ready to consider it, you cannot relive the moment that didn't work. A query letter, on the other hand, sits around until the person you must impress is in a receptive mood. Or so you hope.

# More Advantages of Distance

There's another factor. If your prose is magic but your appearance is poison to the editor, there's little chance that your writing will be given a fair reading. You may be too tall or too short, too warty or too smooth, too young or too old, a buffoon or not funny enough. Worse yet, you may look exactly like the editor's twin brother, the one who got the looks and stole his way to fame. Once seen, you are pegged for life — and your words remain unbought.

Better not to be seen at all, except in sparkling, witty, clear phrases certain to pull thousands of excited new readers to the publication. Then, if a meeting transpires, you have the saving grace of being part of the editor's success. Funny how much better you will look then!

# Written Proof

A final thought: what if the editor says "great, bar no expense" during the personal interview, and you invest precious time and funds to produce a masterpiece. You rush back to the office to deliver the gem and that eager visionary says no, sorry, can't remember the discussion ... Or the editor has left the publication and the replacement, busily wiping the slate, can't find anything on the desk about such a commitment. Such tales dot the freelancing landscape. Keep the queries and commitments in writing, from inception to completion.

You also need a go-ahead in writing to be able to deduct the incurred costs from your income for tax purposes, whether the piece is ultimately bought or rejected. But more on that later.

The best argument against getting an in-person, oral go-ahead is that after granting verbal approval many editors then ask you for a written query!

# 20

# Should You Query Abroad?

For the experienced writer selling abroad can be highly profitable but for newcomers the cost, time delays, and lack of familiarity with the publications themselves usually make the venture unprofitable.

Canada is often the exception, where publication familiarity and ease of accessibility are concerned, since copies of Canadian magazines and even the larger newspapers are available in major U.S. libraries or well stocked news shops, making it possible to study the markets before querying.

Where sample copies are unavailable, you must rely upon the *Writer's Market* listings when attempting to match your ideas with the proper markets. If your query interests the editor, you can usually receive a back issue or two for guidance in manuscript preparation by asking.

## The Other Side of Overseas Sales

I'm speaking from my own experience and that of perhaps 80% of my writing colleagues, who at best dabble at oversea's sales. But there is ample evidence that the foreign market can be extremely lucrative if a writer is able, gutsy, and willing to make some initial investment for a potentially large return.

James Joseph, a widely published professional in the article/book world, best explains how it is done, either at his seminar offered throughout California titled "Writer's World: Inside the Global

Writer's Market" or through an 8-tape series (with workbook and 20 color slides), costing $127, available from him at P.O. Box 24678 Village Station, L.A., CA 90024.

The Joseph system works, but it isn't for the rank amateur nor for the newcomer able to devote only an occasional hour to querying and writing.

# English-language Publications

For those of us primarily focussing on the U.S., I would limit my queries exclusively to English-language publications unless completely fluent in a foreign tongue, including the slang and peculiar regionalisms sometimes needed to write salable copy.

# Stamps

Other countries won't accept U.S. stamps to return your SASE any more than you would accept horse feathers to carry cartage.

Sometimes you can buy stamps of other countries at their embassies or consulates, plus receive a list of current mailing rates. Otherwise, International Reply Coupons are available to guarantee a letter's return, boat mail. For air mail, you need several of them — and they are relatively expensive. (Ask at the Post Office for the current rate and how the coupons are used.)

I usually ask friends travelling to Canada to pick up a stock of stamps for me, but I refuse to use the coupons. Instead, in those rare times I query England, Australia, or New Zealand, I explain the folly of the coupons in my letter and rely upon their good will, and purse, not to reply if they aren't interested in the idea but to let me know if they wish to see the manuscript, deducting the mailing costs from the final payment. If I hear nothing in 60 days, I query elsewhere.

Querying abroad now and then just doesn't work that well, so let me suggest two other approaches, with emphasis on the second:

# Send Manuscripts

I sell "seconds" overseas, pieces that have sold in the U.S. yet have enough appeal to interest readers anywhere. Most of those, for me, are travel or general interest articles.

If a resale takes place, fine. If it doesn't, it is a small gamble since there is little or no rewriting involved. The only costs come from making a photocopy of the original, putting it in an envelope, and sending it boat rate with a cover letter explaining where the item was previously used. I also mention that there are no "rights" difficulties, and why there is no return postage. It might cost $1.50 in shipping and 15 minutes of photocopying and addressing, on the long shot that it will be used abroad and pay from $25-350. Where photos are involved, I include a list of available prints or slides, with a copy of the caption sheets, and ask them to indicate which shots they would like to consider. The editor replies by mail (or sometimes calls), I send the photos, and eventually the payment and the photos come back. Yet there's an easier way.

# Market Through Syndicates

There are sales houses which act as brokers between American writers and hundreds of markets abroad, some in English, many in foreign languages. They find the clients, make the sales pitch, handle the translations, reproduce the slides, and pay you when you least expect it. That nets you about half the income you would have made had you done all the work of generating the sale yourself. It's a bargain at 50%.

See the *Writer's Market* under "syndicates," and, if available at your library, the *Editor and Publisher Syndicate Directory*. Read the write-ups closely to make sure they sell to the types of publications you work. Then either query them or send a full manuscript, with information about illustrations, where the item has already been in print (if it has), and any rights that others have purchased. Almost all of the syndicates listed are U.S.-based or have local offices, so stamps are no problem, and you can use an SASE. (An example of a letter to a syndicate is in Part Seven.)

There's little so pleasing to new writers as receiving a tearsheet or a magazine copy of their work in a language they've never seen written before — with a tidy check attached! Or to receive a quarterly payment sheet with foreign publications listed, plus negotiable tender.

My experience with syndicates has so far been mixed. Some don't reply to queries or acknowledge the receipt of manuscripts, even when contacted later. But most are attentive and quite frank. They reject more items than they accept, usually because the topics won't sell abroad or the photos are unusable. Twice I tried to market items directly that the syndicates had rejected. They were right. The foreign markets, at least those I contacted, weren't interested.

Selling abroad? Concentrate on the U.S. and Canada, and when those sources are exhausted (or you are), check with the syndicates. Later, when your sales are humming at home, check James Joseph's system. And *boa sorte*.

---

*"To an extent, I will judge the writer's ability by the query letter, although I realize in no way does a letter approach the style and in-depth coverage necessary for a full-length feature. Nonetheless, some of the query letters I receive are so poor, if not absurd, that I couldn't possibly make an assignment even if the idea is a good one. Case in point: A few years back an aspiring writer queried me on an article about diabetes. A worthy subject and one in which we might well have been interested. Unfortunately, the writer misspelled "diabetes" on all three occasions the disease was mentioned. How the devil could I even contemplate making an assignment?"*

Bob Kleinfelder, Senior Editor, *The Lion* Magazine (Lions Club International)

# PART THREE

## Query Letters for Books

# 21

## Book Queries

**N**onfiction books, which comprise some 92% of those bought by publishers, are queried before being written in all but a few cases. The exceptions — usually short books (50 pages or less) or juvenile books — are described later.

It makes no sense to write 100 or 500 pages of the last word on (anything) only to find out that nobody wants to publish it. If it's smart to test the article market first with a query letter, so you can wrap the writing around the user's needs, it's 100 times smarter for a book!

But there are a few hitches.

One, the query will probably be two pages long rather than one. Too much to say, usually, for one page. And you can keep it to two, a readable length, by appending supplements.

What kind of items would you attach to, or at least submit with, your longer query? An annotated table of contents or an outline, a one-page synopsis (if necessary), and a reference/resource sheet. Plus an SASE.

## The Book Query

This differs little from the article query in purpose or form, other than being longer and selling a heftier product. You have an idea to sell, your book theme, and a person to sell as its writer, you — sometimes with a co-author or a band of fellow conspirators. Your letter must interest the publisher in financing the venture.

The costs of including your article in a magazine are modest, and are usually covered by the advertising income. But books come less blessed. It costs the publisher anywhere from $3,000-10,000 for a modest run of any book, plus that again for promotion, a chunk more for overhead, 10% or so off the list (retail) price for your royalty, a pile of books as comps to get reviewers and distributors to make your book known about and available, and something (if anything's left) for profit. Mind you, that's their problem — and publishing is a profitable business, almost despite itself.

But it's your problem too when you try to convince an editor to invest that many thousand dollars, on the hope of a profit, in your idea and your prose. Book editors have a lot more questions. And they need a lot more up-front convincing.

So your query and its attachments must be designed to answer most of those questions, put you and your idea in the best professional light, and save you the greatest amount of pre-contract writing time.

Your query must first sell the idea, why others would buy a book to read about it, what is already in print about the topic and why your book would be bought rather than (or in addition to) that available, who specifically would be most interested, how they can be made aware of your book (if that's not obvious), and why you should write it.

Tell the editor of your credentials, expertise, access to others who know the topic well, and/or experience. You needn't have sung in the Met to write a book telling others how to succeed professionally in an operatic career, but you sure in blazes better have some interviews with those who have, either promised or completed, and a long list of practical tips before you even think about that text. And you'd better let the editor know about that pool of applied information.

If you're writing the book with somebody else, tell the editor who is doing what, who is handling the contracting and is the go-between, and just who is that other person anyway. If a committee is writing the book, God forbid, do the same for each.

All that plus the letter must make the topic come alive. It must have the same verve and zest your book will need to keep its readers awake and eager for more. It's a sure bet that if you can't keep a query letter moving and lively for two pages, 200 pages will be lethal. You will be judged by the query. Would you seek a teaching position in the English Department with a letter half-misspelled? Would you ask for $10,000 to finance a book in a letter that is confused and rambling and dull?

# Attachments: The Contents

The query letter sells the idea and you, as well as gives a general explanation of what the book is about. Yet to pass fair judgment, the editor (and a cadre of advisors, at some publishing firms, who must also review the proposal) must know how you will organize the topic.

That is best done by providing an outline or an annotated table of contents.

An outline is easy to envision since every junior high school student is forced to prepare one sometime. It tells, in order, the topic, its main sub-divisions, and their sub-sub-divisions. Usually with Roman numerals, capital letters, numbers — you remember.

Alas, many books don't tightly follow such a rational breakdown. And outlines tend to read and look like a skyscraper's supports in its first stages: thin, rigid, and not much in between.

I prefer an annotated table of contents. It's a table of contents, as if the book were completed, with an annotation — a sentence or two — explaining that chapter and how it relates to the main theme, plus, if necessary, a specific fact or two that adds some excitement to its contents.

# Synopsis

A condensation or summary, in one page. If you can't do it in a page, says the conventional wisdom, you don't have a handle on it. And you can't do it any better in five. What's the book all about? And how are you going to share that with the reader?

Often the synopsis can be given in the query letter, so there is no need to say essentially the same thing again.

If a synopsis is needed, just be sure that enough is said about the topic in the query to snag the editor's interest, then add that the topic will be explained more fully in the synopsis attached.

# Reference/Resource Sheet

This tells the editor, and others interested, where you are getting the book material from! Few are so gifted or positioned that their prose is totally unique — or funneled from some higher source solely through them, claims notwithstanding.

Editors feel comfortable when books contain facts, quotes, and anecdotes that have some known origin. They like history that somebody else has heard about, and people quoted who really existed. So this assures the editor that you are using, at least in part, recorded and known information. And it tells where that information comes from and how you got it.

The **reference** segment tells what recorded (usually written) material was found where. Simply list the most important information in annotated bibliographical fashion, with the annotation a sentence or two telling how that information relates to the theme of the book.

The **resource** segment refers to information that comes from living resources — people. This generally refers to interviews. These are also listed in annotated biographical form. The biography identifies each person and what qualifies them to speak about the topic. The annotation tells how what they say relates to the theme of your book.

This page — it can be longer, if needed — is far more important than it appears. Assuming a solid query, good organization, and a sensible synopsis, you will still be judged strongly by your sources. Does this page show familiarity with the newest research? Are the key names in the field here? Are the streams of wisdom from which you are drawing truly so, or are they weak, seasonal run-offs? Which is worthier of a $10,000 investment?

# The Follow-Up . . . .

Send a dynamic package — query, outline/contents, synopsis, references/resources — to the "best" market, following the 15-step

querying approach used for articles, but expanded and slightly modified. When an eager editor begs for more, indicating that three solid
chapters are all that separate you from a contract and certain glory (not
to mention lucre), get to it. Write those chapters with the same devoted
precision that produced a winning query. Can that fame and fortune be
far behind?

## And Those Few Exceptions?

Sometimes it just isn't worth the effort to produce such a multi-
pieced query, such a lovely selling package, particularly if it's faster to
finish the book itself and just take your chances.

The editors agree, and for very short works (say 50 pages or less)
or for juvenile books (for readers in the lower grades) where the words
are few and the illustrations many, simply prepare the finished product,
attach a cover letter saying what is necessary to effect a sale, and that's
it.

Other kinds of books also follow this form: cartoon books,
anthologies (which can also be queried), humor, and any other publication where the material really has to be seen in final form to be
understood, loved, and published.

Sometimes a book in this category is partially sent, as in Query
Example #9, in Part Six. Some of the text and illustrations are offered,
with the rest promised quickly. But usually it is best to let the editor see
the masterpiece intact.

# Query Example #3

123 Main Street
Carpinteria, CA 93013
(805) 123-4567
Month 1, 1985

Mr. Rolf Zimmerman
Editor, Action Books
2745 Del Vista Blvd.
St. Louis, MO 70000

Dear Mr. Zimmerman:

We need a new sports challenge that any person would be proud to achieve, most could, and all would benefit from trying.

More important, we can launch this event, tell every person how to train for it, and explain to any group or organization how to be its sponsor -- all in a 100-page tome that would put Action Books in the annals of sports history. (It should make you plenty of money too!)

The event and the book would be called Run Your Age! Nothing more complicated: the people run their age. But with a slight modification: it could be run in kilometers or miles, with the young (say 15 or under) limited to running in kilometers only (which are about 5/8 of a mile).

Running is as old as mankind. In the past 15 years, as you know, it has become fashionable for both sexes of all ages to run, for competition, for fun, or for something in between. But the craze is slowing down, the 10-K's are levelling off, and a bit of the sparkle is gone.

For the average person, like myself, a 46-year-old without the time (or serious interest) to train for true competition, it became clear quickly that I'd never win a race, could only get a bit better than I was at my best time, would be fighting to maintain those speeds as I aged, and that one can get a kick out of running just so many races, short or long. Multiply me by the millions, subtract the limited number of fairly new runners each year who still have the awe and dream I/we had when we were a few months or years into the sport, and you will have enough to keep the races running -- and millions more, ex- or occasional racers who still run, but for other reasons.

You see, running is for the swift, or so it has always been. But why? There are two elements at stake: speed and endurance. The longer races, the marathons and the ultra-marathons, put both to their fullest test.

But why not a race that rewards endurance and determination and inner pride but ignores speed, making the only stipulation that the distance travelled must be run, not walked? When tired, one stops, then runs again when ready.

And why not a goal that grows ever more demanding? Nature has made living harder the longer one does it. Why not the same for running? Why not make the goal increase in proportion to one's aging? Running 20 miles when one is 20, and 50 when one is 50?

If that seems backwards it is because we are used to equating strength with youth, so a 20-year-old should be able to run 20 miles far easier than a 50-year-old, 50. Indeed. That's the idea.

People need milestones to measure their worth. Run Your Age! provides a simple milestone, something to work towards, accomplish, and cherish. In a way that a win in a 10-K can't. Running one's age needn't be qualified. Fifty miles is fifty miles, period. But winning a 10-K begs the rest of the story: against whom and how many, when, what terrain, and so on.

I shan't belabor the point much longer. The concept is so simple it either makes sense or it doesn't. Yet I see a large company embracing this idea, making it their own, becoming sponsors of age runs nationwide, and acting as a clearinghouse for a list of all who achieve the goal -- and a distributor of rewards (sweatshirts, plaques, certificates, etc.) to the achievers.

Our task, though, is to make the idea known, through a book. A book I want to write, I'd like you to publish, and I think will make an imprint on America, and then the world. The simple ideas are often the best for in them are the germs of universal truth and challenge all recognize and from which they are inspired.

My own experience. In print 900+ times, mostly in magazines and newspapers, about general interest, travel, humor, and sports -- running, in fact. In addition, I've written five books, edited seven more, own a publishing house, was a dean at the university level twice, directed a city recreation program for three years, organized another, headed the CARE program in parts of Colombia and Ecuador, played professional baseball, and much more. Details, if interested.

And I've run my age. First I ran a mile, then three, then six marathons. And three years back, when two friends told me they had run 40 miles when they were 40, I set out to run 44 one Tuesday morning and did it. I plan to run 47 next year. And I'm proud as a peacock of it -- far more so than the 60 races in which I've competed and, on occasion (when the ranks were full of widows and children), I did well.

The annotated table of contents accompanying this query letter explains, in rough form, what such a book might contain. Since the idea has yet to be in print, and since I'm wide open to suggestions on the breadth of the text -- should it be more specific on preparing to run one's age, should it be a workbook for sponsors on how to run the event, should it be both, should it contain model registration forms, etc. -- it is simply a working outline. Yet in lieu of suggestions or other directions, it is how, at present, I propose writing the book.

The reference/resource sheet is skimpy because the topic is new. Yet there are some guides one might use that would help you see that my proposal is not too far off base. And that I might use in the preparation of my text.

So that's it. Is the idea as exciting to you as it is to me? Do you see it as a book your firm wants to print, Mr. Zimmerman? Or do you see a way that the idea could be presented in an even better book?

Please let me know. Thousands are growing too old to reach their age by foot while we dally!

Many thanks.

Gordon Burgett

(For Action Books, attachment p. 1)

ANNOTATED TABLE OF CONTENTS

Run Your Age!

I. Run Your Own Age?

Explains the concept, why it is being proposed, that it is an open challenge to all, where and when it can be done, the few restrictions (the distance must be run, in miles or kilometers, and no times are recorded), and any anecdotal or historical information encountered to reinforce or explain the concept.

II. How One Prepares.

A general review of the basics of running, drawn from the many texts and references in this field. Who shouldn't attempt the challenge. Of those who should, or could, how they would work up to the level where such a run would be sensible. And then a solid review of the running books now available, in annotated bibliographical fashion, to emphasize the points each makes from which the potential age runners would benefit.

III. The Day of the Event.

How one faces the task, mentally and physically. Pre-run preparation. Needed support. Water stops, aid backups or contacts. A mental framework that will make the task more enjoyable -- or endurable. And what one does when one finishes, on or short of the mark. Post-run rest and recuperation. And how you brag gracefully to your friends!

IV. Sponsoring an Age Run.

Promotion, site selection, route measurement, marking, aid stations, medical and traffic help, necessary approvals, support wagons, water and nutrient stops, washrooms, dressing room and equipment (extra clothes, shoes, Vaseline, etc.) storage, running verification, awards, post-run publicity, etc. Everything but clocks.

(For Action Books, attachment p. 2)

REFERENCE/RESOURCE SHEET

Run Your Age!

## References

There are no direct references from which one can draw information or guidance about this concept since the idea has yet to appear in print. However, from the following books one can find evidence, if it is needed, that running one's age is possible and that the organization of such an event is feasible:

Glasser, William, Positive Addiction, Harper and Row, 1976
Sheehan, George, This Running Life, Simon and Schuster, 1980
Sheehan, George, Running and Being: The Total Experience, Simon and Schuster, 1978
Bloom, Marc, What It Takes To Go The Distance, Holt, Rinehart and Winston, 1981
Sally Edwards, Triathlon, Contemporary Books, 1983
David Montgomery, The Triathlon Handbook, Leisure Press, 1983
Paul Perry, Complete Book of Triathloning, New American Library, 1983

Plus additional marathoning books by Nathan Aaseng, Bob Anderson, Gayle Barron, Richard Benyo, Skip Brown, Gail Campbell, Julianne Fogel, Hal Higdon, John Humphreys, Bill Rodgers, Jim Shapiro, Manfred Steffny, and Cliff Temple.

## Resources

Where references refer to written material, resources (in this case) refer to people I would interview about:

    (1.) the feasibility and advisability of having people run their age
    (2.) the psychological value of having such a goal known to all
    (3.) the logistics of conducting such an event
    (4.) the value and advisability of running the event "on one's own," with one's own backup support, versus doing so at an organized event

In the first case I would interview, if needed, those who have run marathons or ultramarathons, particularly runners 40 and over.

For (2.), if needed, I would pose the question to sociologists, cultural anthropologists, psychologists, and others whose primary interest -- and writing or speaking -- focus on values.

The third resource folk, concerning the logistics of running such an event, would be those who have administered similar running events, such as marathons or ultramarathons, to see what changes this would necessitate from their other events, what guidebooks they used in their own administration, and what advice they would offer.

The fourth category is the most difficult since, to my knowledge, such an event has not been held, thus one has no basis of comparison for such an answer. The question, however, might be posed to all interviewed in categories (1.) through (3.) to see what insights, if any, they might shed on the choice of the best way to run one's age.

# PART FOUR

## Cover Letters

# 22

# What Is a Cover Letter?

A cover letter is a letter one page or longer that accompanies copy already written or photos being submitted. It usually includes information about what is being sent, why, how it might be used, sources consulted for its preparation, special knowledge or preparation one employs in its research and writing, the availability of additional items (like photographs), and other related facts.

That differs from the query letter, which is written to the editor before the copy is prepared.

## When Do You Send a Cover Letter?

Let's say you meet an inventor who is putting the finishing touches on a translating typewriter. He types a letter on the machine in English, pushes a code for any of a dozen languages, and in a few seconds that message is typed in the chosen tongue.

Even better, the inventor is eager to let the world know of his invention!

So you write a query letter to *Ideas International*, a hot new magazine on the stands. The editor is wild for the article! You complete your research, conduct several interviews, take some photos, and zip the copy his way.

He knows the manuscript is coming, so you don't need a cover letter for that purpose. But you do have to include some comments about the use of the photos; you think you should divulge the origin of some of the more bizarre facts; and you want to be sure that the typesetter spells the inventor's first name "Roberrt" correctly — so you send a cover letter with the copy.

Thus it's possible that you could send both a query and a cover letter to the same editor.

But it's far more likely that a cover letter will accompany material for which there is no query. For fiction, a cover letter might be sent with a short story or a novel. For nonfiction, cover letters often accompany simultaneous, direct, or syndicated submissions, reprints, fillers, or photos.

## To Whom Should the Cover Letter Be Sent?

To the editor or person who would be the most appropriate recipient of the item accompanying the cover letter. If a query letter preceded the manuscript and cover letter submission, it would be sent to the same person indicated in or responding to the query.

When the material and the cover letter are being submitted for the first time, check the current issue of *Writer's Market* and send your items to the appropriate editor.

## What Does a Cover Letter Look Like?

It's a business letter not dissimilar in appearance to a query letter. For form, refer to Chapter 28. A cover letter's contents depend upon why it is being sent, and are better discussed under the various categories that follow. Yet all cover letters must be well written, clear, grammatically proper, and with correct spelling — in every way the best possible demonstration of your writing ability.

Remember, the editor has relatively little evidence of your writing. You've previously sent a query letter, perhaps. Or only the copy attached to the cover letter. From those limited examples the editor must decide whether to purchase your prose.

You could flood that editor's mail with other examples, of course, but that wouldn't do. Just make sure that every item you put before his or her eyes displays your writing skills in the best professional light. Why? Because a well written article accompanied by a poorly written cover letter — creative spelling, crazy asides, grammar from another planet — may well be rejected. It simply raises too many doubts in the editor's mind.

## Can You Send Simultaneous Cover Letters?

Sure. If you are sending simultaneous submissions or reprints you can produce a master letter and send copies with each submission or reprint. We'll dwell on each of these categories below, and will suggest times when simultaneous cover letters, while proper, might be more effective if replaced by a personal cover note.

# 23

## Simultaneous Submission Cover Letters

Simultaneous submissions can usually be sent to editors of newspaper travel sections or of weekly newspaper supplements, as well as to editors of in-flight, religious, or regional magazines. The rule-of-thumb is that you cannot send the same submission to publications whose circulation, distribution, or readership overlap.

## Newspaper Travel Cover Letter

In newspaper travel, for example, you could send the same item to, say, the *Los Angeles Times*, the *Chicago Tribune*, and *Newsday*, on Long Island, since none comes close to overlapping another. But you could not send it to the *Wall Street Journal* or the *Christian Science Monitor*, for example, and any other newspaper, since the *Journal* and *Monitor* are national and overlap all others.

Querying here seldom works because travel editors are too busy to play the correspondence game. If you have a travel item or article you think their readers would enjoy, send it, with an SASE. Then forget it. Newspaper travel pays on publication, which can be a week or a year after receipt of your copy.

The pay in newspaper travel for copy without photos is modest, $80-125 or so. But you can make a dozen copies of an article (best lenghth, 1000-1500 words) and send them to scattered newspapers at the same time. The chance of selling the piece three or four times offsets the pay range and the risk of submitting without a go-ahead from a query.

Let's say that you have written an electric 1400-word gem, a travel piece so good that you are sure editors will stop the press to put it in the earliest possible edition! And you decide to give the lucky millions in L.A., Chicago, and the greater New York City area the chance to see this prose in their local newspapers.

So you might prepare a cover letter that would read as follows:

### Cover Example #1

GORDON BURGETT
123 Main Street
Carpinteria, CA 93013
(805) 123-4567

Dear Mr. Johnson:

"Where The Westerns Were Born and the Stars Now Hide" can only be Santa Barbara, California, site of the earliest Flying A shoot-em-ups and the hidden haven, in its secluded canyons and Montecito niches, of many of today's top film, stage, and concert stars. The 1,400-word article, attached, tells your readers how to find the remnants of the Flying A, where the stars come out at night, and how they can blend the resort's natural bounty of surf, sun, and wilderness with the well-preserved relics of a rich historic past, fine cuisine, and a thriving night life.

I also have about 100 good-to-excellent b/w's to select from, if interested. Let me know and I'll send the 16 best, for your choice. (Also available, 36 slides so alluring you will want to abandon the New York tundra on the spot!)

Please don't return the ms, just your verdict in the SASE.

Thanks,

*Gordon Burgett*

So you make three clean copies of each page of your manuscript, collate them, and find three manila envelopes into which you insert an unfolded article and an SASE for each editor.

Do you need a cover letter? Isn't it obvious why the contents are being sent? Won't the SASE get the response you desire?

If you have nothing more to say, a cover letter isn't mandatory. You could simply mail the material and wait for the money truck.

But why not take every advantage to sell your prose and other, related income stretchers? Why half-sell when a note could make a major difference, perhaps even double the editor's ante?

# Suggested Format

Let's say that your magic prose concerns Santa Barbara, California, and you are sending this to *Newsday*'s travel editor. Further, that you have taken both black/white photos and color slides.

I write this cover letter on pre-cut paper that is only 5" long. (It can be 8.5" wide or less.) It is stapled as the first page on top of the actual manuscript, and covers only the title, the by-line, and the word count. (I staple newspaper submissions but send magazine submissions paperclipped. The first are simply treated with less care so I want to make certain that all the pages stay together.)

That is, I don't begin the actual copy until at least the middle of the first page of the manuscript. In that way the editor will read my cover note first and will be so enchanted by my summary of the article's contents and the promise of eye-boggling photos that he/she will continue reading the manuscript that begins where my note ends. The natural conclusion would be a quick note (probably on the back of my cover letter) to send the b/w's as soon as possible, mailed that day in my SASE. (I would respond the moment the request was received lest the Long Islanders be deprived of this article even one hour longer than absolutely necessary.)

Note the contents of the cover letter. My address, phone, and the date appear at the top. The phone makes me instantly accessible if the editor has a question or wants the material with undue haste.

The first paragraph describes the article attached, in much the same tone as the copy itself. If the piece is humorous or light, so is the opening. If it's somber or heavily factual, that first paragraph follows suit.

The opening paragraph is what sells your copy. If you can't ignite a spark of interest and highlight the key factor(s) in your piece in those first words, the editor may simply set it aside. So the opener, like the lead in an article, must tickle that interest and make the editor want to read more.

The second paragraph tells what photos you have for sale and how you will make them available to the editor. Since black-and-whites are by far the most sought by newspaper travel editors, mention them first. You don't want to tie up all of your photos with one editor, so offer to send a selection, say 16, or even the five best.

Should you have a photo so noteworthy it may rival the copy for inclusion on the travel page, you may wish to expand upon it in the second paragraph. A shot of a housewife watching in awe as her dime slot machine belches out $5,000 might highlight a piece on hitting the gambling meccas in New Jersey or Nevada.

The third paragraph is a personal preference. It strikes me as unpatriotic to make my uncle, Sam, unduly fat from postal proceeds from returning unusable manuscripts. Why pay to get a rejection back when it will be folded and bent so badly it can't be sent to another editor? Rather, a single first-class stamp on a small envelope gets the reply I need.

There's another way that's even less expensive and just as effective to get a reply. Include a self-addressed, stamped postcard with boxes to check and a space on the bottom for comments and editor identification. The boxes might say:

Submission: _____

\_\_\_\_ I'm holding for possible future use.
\_\_\_\_ Let's see your b/w photos.
\_\_\_\_ Let's see your slides.
\_\_\_\_ Not this time!

Comments:


Name_____
Publication_____


# Are These Individually Written?

The first time you are mailing to various newspaper travel sections and you don't know the editors' names, you can write a general cover letter, making certain not to distinguish it with geographic or specific comments. Note that the example mentions New York and includes the editor's name. In the general note you would address it to Dear Travel Editor — and omit such specifics. (You will know the editor's names from the responses to this first mailing!)

But it makes more sense to prepare the travel cover letters for each editor, and attach them to the manuscripts that are mass produced. Editors are people too, and, like you, they respond better when called by a name and spoken to directly. And over time you will come to know them, indirectly, and will have particular comments to add.

It's easy enough to write a master cover letter, circle each item that must be personalized, and type these up quickly or program them into your word processor, with inserts.

# Final Thoughts About Newspaper Travel Cover Letters

These are kept short because the copy is attached. It's obvious why the material is being sent (you want fame and fortune by having it appear in the newspaper) and how it might be used. The sources consulted and special skills you brought to it are also less important: the editor can read it to see if its content is acceptable.

The note here is sent to provide a short selling summary and to interest the editor in other support items for sale, like photos. Keep it interesting, quick, and to the point.

# Do You Use This Short Form for Other Simultaneous Submissions?

No, because it is designed to meet the needs of    newspaper submissions. Its brevity works particularly well in this case, and most other cover letters simply need more words to do more things. In fact, it won't always work even for the cases we've cited in this section. When they too require more space than it affords, a full-page letter is advised.

# Other Simultaneous Submission Cover Letters

The form of cover letter described for submission to newspaper travel editors won't usually work for the other major types of simultaneous submissions: newspaper weekly supplements and in-flight, regional, or religious magazines.

# Newspaper Weekly Supplements

These are generally the magazine-like inserts distributed with newspapers, usually on Saturday or Sunday. Some, like *Parade Magazine* or *Family Weekly*, are national in distribution, though they appear in the local newspaper. Others are produced by a newspaper itself, like the *Dallas Life Magazine* (the Sunday magazine of *The Dallas Morning News*) and *The Nevadan* (the Sunday magazine of *The Las Vegas Review Journal*).

If the copy is sent to a national supplement it cannot be submitted, unless rejected, to another national or local supplement, since one must limit simultaneous submissions to newspapers that do not overlap in circulation or distribution.

Yet if one restricts submission to local supplements only, and these are sufficiently far apart, the process is not unlike that used for newspaper travel.

A full-page letter is probably more appropriate here since the cover may well require more content. It should also be individually written, much as one would do with higher-paying magazine submissions.

The contents of the letter depend entirely on what needs to be said about the accompanying copy. How or why it might interest local readers usually has highest priority with the editor, for local weekly supplements are overwhelmingly interested in local or regional matters.

The way one circumvents this difficulty, if hoping to distribute the same piece nationwide, is by focussing the article on an universal topic that appeals to residents everywhere. Editors are particularly receptive to humor or humorous pieces when the topic is so broad.

The letter might explain the origin of the material cited, the author's expertise for discussing the topic, the availability of illustrations or photos, or other matters that would help sell the copy.

Again, the writing in the cover letter and the overall professionalism in its composition is extremely important. The editor will read the cover letter first. Will that editor even bother to look at the attachment if the cover letter looks like it was composed by an illiterate or a reveller in search of sobriety?

While most newspaper supplement editors will assume that you are submitting your article to other, similar publications outside of their orb, you can either indicate SIMULTANEOUS SUBMISSION on the manuscript below the word count (on the upper right-hand corner of the first page) or you can explain this in the cover letter.

## Magazine Simultaneous Submissions: In-Flight, Regional, and Religious

In general what has been said about newspaper travel and weekly supplements concerning where and when simultaneous submissions can be sent applies to these three magazine categories as well.

One can send the same manuscript to in-flight magazines that do not overlap — that is, whose airlines do not serve the same geographic area. So regional lines each serving the Northeast, Alaska, Mexico, the South, and Hawaii could be sent the same item, but you could not send it to a national or world carrier, say to United or Pan American, and any other serving the same markets at the same time.

The same holds true for regional magazines. A piece on the name "Portland" could be sold to regional magazines in Oregon and Maine, but not simultaneously to a national with readership in either or both states.

Religious magazines generally feel that their readership comes from their own flock, so if you could find a topic — God knows what! — that would appeal to, say, the Dunkards, Unitarians, Mormons, and the Hardshell Doubters, you could send it a publication of each of those sects or faiths. But if the HD's have five magazines, you must send it to each one at a time since their readership does indeed overlap.

Mind you, it is important to check the current *Writer's Market* to see if each of the publications in the three fields being discussed does in fact buy simultaneous submissions. Unless it states to the contrary, assume that they do.

Again, the contents of the cover letter accompanying your copy will differ according to the needs that letter must meet or express. The letters should be written individually on full paper, and the editors receiving each will have at least one key question: why would my readers be interested in this topic?

It is imperative that manuscripts that are simultaneously submitted to magazines clearly state the words SIMULTANEOUS SUBMISSION. If necessary, you can either further delineate the breakdown at that point — such as "Dunkard copy," "Northwestern U.S. copy," or "Hawaiian airlines copy" — or you can explain that delineation in the text of the cover letter itself.

As with all submissions or queries, an SASE should accompany the items sent.

# 24

# Reprints

**R**eprints are the reuse of copy already in print, in its original form or slightly modified.

That is, you sold a manuscript to a publication on a first rights basis. It appeared in print, and you submit it to one or many other publications, one at a time or simultaneously, to be reprinted. (It can be sent to many markets because there is no exclusivity in the use of reprints.)

When you submit it as a reprint you have three obligations. You must tell which publication bought the first rights, when it appeared in print in that publication, and that you are offering the editor to whom it is being sent either reprint or second rights. (The terms are interchangeable; there are no third or fourth rights.)

And that's it. The rest the editor should know. That there is no exclusivity, that you can offer it to the competition, that it may have been read by that publication's readership elsewhere, that you have already been paid once for this journalistic jewel and you hope to be paid many times more for the same display of literary dexterity.

## What Should a Reprint Submission Cover Letter Contain?

Enough to fulfill your obligation and get the piece bought.

Since the original manuscript must be in print before reprints can be offered for purchase by other editors, why not take a copy of that published original, cut and paste it up so it can be presentably copied, and make as many clean copies as you wish to hawk?

Then send that copy of the article with your cover letter, letting the cover letter refer to the printed sample while it expands on the virtues of its contents and composition, tells the rights being offered, mentions the availability of photos or slides, and suggests that a copy can be sent for their typesetter's ease, as this example shows:

## Cover Example #2

123 Main Street
Carpinteria, CA 93013
(805) 123-4567
Month 1, 1985

Mrs. Bernice Elston
Articles Editor, Spring News
666 Albatross Avenue
Burlington Jct., MO 60000

Dear Ms Elston:

How many of your readers are certain that they could write better greeting cards than those on the racks? How many would like to earn $60 or $70 for just writing the lines?

The enclosed article tells them how to prepare and sell their own ideas to the major U.S. firms that buy from the public.

It discusses what is being bought, which companies are currently buying, how they should be approached, and when to submit seasonals and everyday cards. Even more crucial, it tells what the cards must contain, the three-word magic formula, and why some cards sell while others don't.

Editors from three top companies are quoted, anecdotes about freelance writers are included, the facts are current, and the box following the prose lists the top 20 markets, each with an address, the editor's name, and the kinds of cards each firm prefers.

Most important, since humor is what most greeting card editors want, humor is what this piece offers, consistently and gently. But the contents are serious: I've sold hundreds of comedy lines, to virtually every company listed (though most to Hallmark), so I know that you can laugh while you write but it takes diligence and purpose to sell.

The article enclosed first appeared in the <u>Nordvelt</u> <u>Airline</u> <u>News</u> in May, 1983, so I am offering you second rights.  The photos and the greeting card illustrations were sold on a one-time rights basis, and are available for you to use again.  I also have 24 additional slides and an assortment of 40 cards from which you could select other illustrations, if interested.

It is difficult to edit or typeset from a printed article so should you wish to publish this piece I'll gladly send you a copy of the original, double-spaced manuscript.  Just let me know.

A nebbish on the outside of the card shouts, "You're a saint!  History will immortalize you for the contribution you're making to society ...

... by laughing at these stupid cards!" finishes the inside.

The fun and funds somebody earned by writing and submitting that line, seeing it appear at the store, and even sending it to friends could be shared by many of your readers.  Shall we tell them how?

Gordon Burgett

# Why Use This Kind of Letter?

Editors are busy and this gets your task done quickly with the greatest amount of both sales appeal and follow-up acumen.

Starting off with a paragraph or several that summarize the contents and purpose of the article, written in the style or tone of the actual prose, gets right to it. You answer the questions the editor has: why are you writing me, what does the attached item contain, why should I (and my readers) care, and is it worth my time to read?

So make the opening paragraph(s) good reading, concerning a subject the editor's readers care about, written with enthusiasm and an economy of words, and sufficiently alluring so the editor will want to read the whole article.

The short paragraph that follows tells the terms. The article first appeared in such-and-such publication on "x" date (article copy enclosed) and you are offering second (or reprint) rights for its use.

Those three elements are mandatory — but no more are needed. You don't have to reveal that you are also offering it to 732 other publications. That the first editor barely bought it — after 17 rewrites. Or that the reprint, if bought, will pay more than the original sale!

If prints or slides are available — you have them or can get them — an additional paragraph mentioning that can add substantially to your coffers and to the material's desirability. Since illustrative material is usually sold on a "one-time rights" basis, and its purchase with the original manuscript used up those rights, you can offer the same items for sale again, as well as other items the first editor wasn't wise or greedy enough to gobble up with your original sale.

Tell of the availability of your prints, slides, maps, charts, whatever. If any are particularly good or vital, expand upon them: their quality, uniqueness, crucial importance to understanding the text. And offer to send them for the editor's review for possible purchase with the copy.

The final paragraph seems harmless enough. You offer to send a copy of the original manuscript — double-spaced, wide left margin — for the typesetter's benefit since it would be far easier to use than the folded and tight-spaced article copy sent with the cover letter.

Compassion aside, that lets you keep an eye on those publications most likely to reuse your prose. Editors requesting a copy of the manuscript will as often as not put it into print. Which should mean more, welcome funds find their way into your pocket. Yet the publications most likely to use reprints are, sadly, those most likely not to pay, at least quickly. So by knowing where your words are most likely to appear, you know where to cast an occasional eye on the newsstand or at the library to see if your item saw light, so a gentle reminder of non- or slow payment might be sent.

Most "pay on publication" magazines do just that, promptly. But if a month has passed since the item appeared in print, I'd drop the editor a note complimenting the good job done with your piece in the recent issue. Find something to commend. Then note that the check was likely mailed but has yet to arrive. Thank the editor for using your piece. A month later and no check, forget the compliments!

# Who Buys Reprints?

Any publication can buy reprints but the higher priced ones seldom do. And if a publication pays on acceptance, it's to your advantage to query and prepare an original manuscript when you receive a positive response to your query, as the professionals do.

But those that pay on publication are ideal for reprint submissions. Professionals don't query them. It's not worth the time for such a vague and delayed possibility of use and payment. But items already sold that lend themselves to resale are indeed worth the time and effort to market this way. All the better, almost all "pay on publication" markets seek and buy reprints.

# How Do Reprints Differ From Simultaneous Submissions?

In one sense reprints can be simultaneous submissions. Once the item has appeared in print you can market it simultaneously, if you wish, since it has no exclusivity and your cover letter will indicate that it is a reprint (or for second rights).

But it differs from newspaper and magazine simultaneous submissions, as mentioned elsewhere in this section, because with reprints the copy has already appeared in print, locally or nationally. What you are offering the editor is the opportunity to use it again, without regard to possible market overlap. That is the editor's concern as long as you have clearly indicated that what you are selling is a reprint or for second rights. Nor should you mark "simultaneous submission" on the manuscript.

# How Much Do They Pay for Reprints?

This varies according to the purchaser, but it's almost always less than that for the original manuscript, often 75% or even 50% of the rate of first-appearance material.

With photos or illustrations, though, you can often equal and sometimes surpass the amount paid for an original.

# Will Rewriting a Reprint Increase Its Value?

Usually, but it also increases your working time, so the question for you is whether the extra minutes or hours compensate for the increase in pay. Especially since your markets will likely pay on publication, meaning that if they use the item at all your pay will be longer in coming.

If the editor will use the item only if it is rewritten, you must decide if it's worth doing based primarily on those criteria. Sometimes it's possible to get a firm commitment from a "pay on publication" editor that either the piece will indeed be used or that you will, in that particular case, be paid upon its acceptance.

# Can You Send the Same Letter to Every Editor?

The same basic copy, yes. I'd change the name in the greeting, of course. Editors are so human they like to be addressed by their own names!

Where you know that a publication has specific needs that your copy addresses, you might change your cover letter to reflect that. If you know that an editor, for example, eagerly seeks good slides for his cover to match the key story, you might well mention some particularly good slides that could serve. If your piece would be of interest to octologists or octogenarians, and your editors cater to those readers, draw attention to the tie-in between what you wrote and what they read.

But otherwise a dynamite letter well directed to even the crustiest of editors should blast loose the rustiest of purselocks. A solid sales letter promoting good, needed copy, even secondhand, should be altered only when the changes make it an even better sales tool.

## Is There a Difference Between Reprints and Second Rights?

Only a semantical difference; they refer to precisely the same thing. A reprint sometimes refers to an article or printed item being an absolute or near-exact copy of an original. But when one refers to rights they are identical: reprint rights and second rights are the same.

# 25

## Fillers

**M**ost fillers are short items produced in manuscript form with the word "filler" written under the word count in the upper right-hand corner of the first page. They are sent with an SASE to the Filler Editor. Few require a cover letter.

After all, the Filler Editor (if such a person actually exists) knows what you want: to be paid a king's ransom for a short gem or several paragraphs of wit or clarion insight.

So send a cover letter only in those rare cases where it is necessary to say something more than (1) I am enclosing a nearly priceless piece of writing, (2) please pay me top price for it nevertheless, (3) instantly, and (4) let me know your decision even sooner!

When might a cover letter be necessary with a filler? In one of the following instances:

(1.) The item includes information not well known or subject to question by the editor. You can cite the source in a cover letter or even at the end of the material itself. If it's truly shocking you might even make a copy of the source and include that as part of or attached to the cover letter;

(2.) You can provide photos or illustrative material related to the filler. That too could either be noted on the filler itself or explained, probably in greater detail, in the cover letter;

(3.) You want to offer additional information about the filler or related fillers. For example, that you could expand on the item for a full article or that you could provide other such items regularly or as a column if the editor is interested, or

(4.) Any other comments that must be made concerning the filler or fillers that would more properly done in an accompanying letter.

If a cover letter isn't necessary, just send in the copy. A superfluous letter costs postage, uses up the editor's time, reflects poorly on your wisdom, and detracts from the only true purpose of your submission, selling your short filler gem.

# 26

## Syndication

The lines between a query letter and a cover letter grow fuzzy in this category, as they do when you submit children's or very short fiction (described elsewhere).

In a query, you send the letter before you write the material; in a cover letter, after.

So in some ways you do both when contacting a syndicate.

A bit of background first will make this clearer. Instead of writing an article and submitting it directly to an editor or, better yet, querying and writing once you have a go-ahead, with a manuscript submission at that point, a syndicate is a broker, a go-between, who receives your material and sells it to one or several publications.

Most syndicates work the domestic market, with an occasional sale abroad. Some work outside the U.S. exclusively. Some buy single features and/or serials. Many prefer on-going columns.

So you must study your markets in the current *Writer's Market* or the *Editor and Publisher Syndicate Directory*, and submit according to their needs and your interests.

## Single Features

Single features, or even a series of several items about the same topic, are bought, but less often or widely than columns. How you submit to syndicates with these items depends upon whether the material is new or is being offered for reprint.

If you wish to sell an article or series that is new, that you have never had published in that form or perhaps even written, you can either follow the standard querying approach or you can do the actual writing and send the copy to the syndicate. The query or cover letter will be the same as any other such letter with the exception that the wording will discuss syndication rather than single market submission. Another obvious deviation: why would many markets be interested in this topic?

# Article Reprints

If you have already sold one or several articles, say in the United States and Canada, and you think that markets outside of North America would also be interested in that material, you can send them, singly or together, to syndicates that work such publications abroad.

In this case your cover letter will differ little from a standard reprint cover letter, except that you must indicate all of the publications that have used the article(s) and offer either overseas rights or those for a particular area or language to the syndication.

Syndicates working the foreign markets are particularly interested in your prints and slides, so be explicit here: precisely what you have, number and quality.

You might also ask, in a querying fashion, if there are other topics they are seeking at the present time. Finally, cover letters to syndicates often contain more information, thus need more space. The one-page guideline for most such letters usually need to be relaxed here, to take care of all the business in one writing.

# Columns

Columns are where the query and cover letter become one.

Most syndication editors want to see a selection of columns, six or ten in number ranging from 500-1000 words long, to evaluate your writing skills and to have a similar offering to show prospective clients among the newspapers and occasional magazines that the syndicate serves, who want to make the same evaluation.

Furthermore, should an agreement be reached that calls for your provision of a new column on a daily, weekly, or monthly basis, the syndicate wants at least some early indication that you can indeed write about the same general theme from six or ten different approaches. And, finally, should you not live up to your part of the agreement or even fall behind schedule, a well of 6-10 columns can be drawn from to temporarily fill the gap.

What you send with those first samples concerns us here.

Since the sample columns accompany your first letter, it is a cover letter. But it is also a query, since its purpose is to sell your idea (a new column) and yourself (as the writer of the columns). The sample columns show how you would approach the idea and what writing skills you bring to the task. And the crucial question is whether that syndicate will represent you in the sale of those literary jewels — and the thousands to come — so they can be read by the masses everywhere.

Thus the letter does what a query must do. It must sell your idea and you. And to do that it must be written as well as the items to be sold. It must:

(1.) explain your column concept clearly
(2.) tell why readers would want to know about it
(3.) indicate which readers would be particularly interested
(4.) list other columns or information now available about the topic to them
(5.) tell how your column will provide that information better: more current, easier to understand and apply, wittier, drawn from wider sources, etc.
(6.) explain your credentials and how they relate to this column
(7.) list your publications and other evidences of idea dissemination, emphasizing those most closely related to the column idea
(8.) indicate any following you or your publications have among professional peers, laymen, or others likely to be drawn to the column for that reason

(9.) show a keen interest in writing the column and how it can be worked into your already busy professional schedule so that deadlines will be faithfully met

(10.) plus anything else needed to sell your idea and you as the person to bring it to the public in print through their syndicate.

How long should this query/cover letter be? Long enough to get you in every publication possible, but short enough to do all its tasks briskly, fully, and — most important — convincingly. A page or two, probably, with attachments, if necessary. Plus those columns. Both must shine. A super letter and lousy columns will be as effective as super columns and a lousy letter. Which do you believe? Make both work and Royko and Bombeck are in big trouble!

# 27

## Other Cover Letters

## Photos and Illustrations

The discussion of photos and illustrations (drawings, maps, charts, etc.) in this book concerns only those submitted with or supplementary to written copy, such as prints or slides with a travel article, diagrams for a book, or a cover shot in conjunction with an article.

Discussion of other uses and the means of submission of photos are best left to the respective professional fields and their how-to journals of marketing, or the *Photographer's Market.*

In most cases you would simply mention their availability in a query letter, indicating the kind, quantity, and perhaps something about the quality of the photos or illustrative materials, then offer to send the items, if interested, for the editor's perusal and selection with your manuscript. Sometimes an item of particular importance, or uniqueness, will be described in greater detail. Some even send a proof, as an example.

Cover letters might be sent about photos or illustrations in two cases:

(1.) As a paragraph or segment of the cover note or letter, containing comments similar to those in the query described above, to newspaper travel simultaneous submission markets, syndicates, or reprint buyers, or

(2.) As a special note to editors buying fillers or with an actual manuscript, previously queried, when submitted or if delayed. In this case there would have to be something of unusual worth about the photo or illustration to bring to the editor's attention.

For example, while preparing a piece on *pelota de guante* in Quito you capture an extraordinary shot of the ball striking a rare bird in flight. Or you have a time sequence showing a patch of forest being destroyed by the flow of lava from a fresh volcano. You were able to take photos of five TV stars while interviewing John Travolta, or you have access to a photo showing an 800-pound safe being suspended from a coated piece of paper which you mention in a cover note accompanying a filler about a new substance that triples the tensile strength of cloth.

The rationale for the cover letter or note is that the photos or illustrations will make the copy even more valuable to the editor — and yourself.

# Delayed Submissions

At times, though rarely, copy requested from a query letter must be submitted after the deadline. In those cases a cover letter is generally required.

Three weeks is the rule-of-thumb submission deadline from the date a query receives a go-ahead. But editors are often more specific, stating an exact date by which the copy must be submitted, sooner if it's urgent, later than three weeks if its ultimate use is in the more distant future.

Let's say that the editor does give you a three-week deadline. All goes well until your principal interview falls through. Benny Henny has been called to the Upper Xingu to save a collapsing bridge. He won't be back for 10 days, and he is the stanchion supporting your article. Worse yet, the interview could only be scheduled four days before that deadline!

In this case a quick call to the editor is necessary, to explain the dilemma and to ask for a two- or three-week delay in the original schedule.

Then, when you actually submit the manuscript, a cover letter might be advisable. In it you would remind the editor of the reason for the delay, your phone conversation, and how you believe that the inconvenience actually resulted in a better article, as much as you dislike having to extend deadlines. While you're at it, ask if a sidebar or box wouldn't be an interesting insight into how an expert like Mr. Henny solves unusual problems in such distant places on such short notice.

The real purpose of the cover with a delayed submission: to remind the editor why it is delayed. Yet if you can honestly turn that delay, and letter, into a strengthening tool, and a means of expanding your print exposure, great.

Need I say that, as with all writing you display for editors, the cover letter should be top-flight prose well stated, brief, accurate, and designed to cement in that editor's mind that you can write?

# Direct Submissions

## Humor

This is the *Mad Magazine* variety, written to be funny, and unqueriable. What would you say in the query, "Do you want to read something funny?" And what could the editor say back but, "Send it to me so I can see if it makes me laugh!"

So common sense says that it should be sent straight in, unadorned and unaccompanied, so as not to draw from the laughs.

Yet there can be exceptions. Sometimes it may not be apparent why the readers would find the topic interesting, even if it is funny. You know why, so the cover letter informs the editor.

You may be aware of something about to occur that will touch the editor's readers, and why your humor piece will be especially timely when published. Your letter tips the editor off.

At times your humor could be even funnier, if that's possible, by including cartoons or comic illustrations — and even more amazing, if that too is possible, you just happen to know *the* person who produces those magic laugh-multipliers. Tell the editor, include a few examples, and either give the person's address or offer to provide both the illustrations and the other person's written permission for their use.

These are the most obvious reasons why a cover letter might accompany non-queried humor. There may be more. But the reasons had better be legitimate. It's best not to distract from the humor itself with needless add-on's. Useless correspondence will leave you with egg on your face. The yoke will be on you.

## Novels

Novels, like short stories, are best sent straight in, without attachments or cover letters, unless it is imperative that the editor know more than can already be guessed: you want to sell the tome, you wrote it, some of the facts are based on actual events, and so on . . . .

A few publishers want to read every word, and thus want you to submit the entire manuscript; others prefer sample chapters (often three), sometimes with a synopsis. List the publishing houses selling novels similar to yours. Librarians are you best friends here. Put those publishers in the order in which you want them to consider your book, and follow their instructions on what to send. The book publishers section in the current *Writer's Market* tells all.

You might send a cover letter with the material in the following cases (and others where it is to your specific advantage):

(1.) If you've been in print often and impressively. Editors prefer to deal with professionals rather than newcomers — usually. A track record says that you can be depended upon to produce what's contracted — usually. And that you'll be more supple when it comes to rewrites — usually.

(2.) If your novel relies heavily on fact. A cover letter should indicate the primary sources used in compiling those facts, and offer to substantiate all critical points, if necessary.

(3.) If your novel talks about actual people, living or dead, where you got your information, quotes, and opinions — and how one can verify that should libel be a consideration.

(4.) If you have expertise in a field that is drawn upon in the novel. Explain your credentials, experience, or whatever the editor should know to be convinced of your understanding of the topic — and offer to prove all claims made, if necessary.

(5.) If your novel is co-authored you must explain whether you are representing both yourself and the other author, and indicate or show some signed authorization to do so, or that each must be contracted separately.

(6.) If to understand your novel the editor must know certain facts or conditions beforehand (that become evident in the unfolding of the text), those should be explained, briefly, so the selected chapters make sense.

(7.) If your novel concerns a subject about to "explode" on the public, one that will elicit wide public attention (or even more limited but profound interest among a particular group), mention that, how you know, and when this explosion is likely to occur.

(8.) If your novel will have particular sales appeal abroad — in a country or region — and that isn't apparent, explain why that is so and how you know.

(9.) Plus any other information that will help sell your book, should it be published, that the editor and the sales division can't readily guess.

## Short Stories

Most editors who buy short stories — a diminishing breed (in number, not size) — simply want to read the stories. If the stories don't work, if they are aimless vignettes or artless ditties or babble inchoate, the editors haven't time to care about the author, the story's background, what is trying to be said, or the rest of it. The material is unusable.

So your first task is to write well, then find a publication that uses short stories. The next step is to submit your best work. Prayer for some will follow. Others call upon patience, *vino*, or more writing, relying on those much relied upon odds to offset editorial insensitivity to the recognition of true genius.

Where does the cover letter fit in? Seldom. A direct submission rarely needs an accompanying letter, just an SASE. The editor can see that what is being sent is a short story. Presumably you want to be paid, and informed if the gem(s) will be published, returned, or fed to livestock.

A cover letter might be sent if you sold to that publication before — editors too have lapses of memory, or new editors replace the old. Or if the subject so hinges on the correctness of some specific knowledge and you feel it imperative to tell how you know the facts. Or other details: you are offering a reprint; this is the core story, never sold, from which your current script is being filmed starring Robert Redford and Loretta Young; this is a translation, now in public domain, of a piece by Brazil's greatest short story writer, Machado de Assis, and so on.

There are times when cover letters accompany short stories, but those are few and the causes are exceptional. If the editor likes the work and has questions, be certain those will be asked. Just let the editor get to like the story first.

# PART FIVE

## Common Ground

# 28

## The Components of a Query or Cover Letter

**Q**uery and cover letters are business letters, and business letters too often are clean, quick, and bland. You want to change the blandness, particularly in the query. It should display the kind of writing you promise to use in the article: exciting, direct, crisp — the reverse of bland. In both keep the quick and clean.

## Format

Most business letters use some form of the block format. In the complete block form, all elements, including the heading and the signature block, line up along the left-hand margin.

In the example of a query letter below (typical of all query letters I write) I use a modified block form. Note the three exceptions from the full block format. The return address (in lieu of a letterhead) and the date (both, parts of the heading), as well as the signature block, are lined up along an imaginary line drawn vertically to the right of the center of the letter's body. The body of the letter in either form is single-spaced except between paragraphs, which are set off by double-spacing instead of indentation. Spacing of the other elements can be seen in the example.

I follow the same modified form in all full cover letters. Shorter cover notes are simplified, as can be seen in the example on Part Seven.

*Heading*                     *(Space*          123 Main Street
                           *optional)*____ Carpinteria, CA 93013
                                             (805) 123-4567
                                             Month 1, Year
                           *(3 spaces)*          •
                                                 •
                                                 •
Mr. Harry Smith                                  •
Editor, <u>The Smith</u>                         •   *Inside Address*
5 Beekman St.                                    •
New York, NY 10038                               •
                           *(2 spaces)*          •
                                                 •
Dear Mr. Smith:                                  •   *Salutation*
                           *(2 spaces)*          •
                                                 •
XXXXXXXXXXXXXXXXXXXXXXXXXXXXXXXXXXXXXXXXXXXXXXXXXXXXXXXXXXXXXX
XXXXXXXXXXXXXXXXXXXXXXXXXXXXXXXXXXXXXXXXXXXXXXXXXXXXXXXXXXXXX
XXXXXXXXXXXXXXXXXXXXX.
                           *(1 space)*
XXXXXXXXXXXXXXXXXXXXXXXXXXXXXXXXXXXXXXXXXXXXXXXXXXXXXXXXXXXXXXX!
                           *(1 space)*
XXXXXXXXXXXXXXXXXXXXXXXXXXXXXXXXXXXXXXXXXXXXXXXXXXXXXXXXXXXXXXXX
XXXXXXXXXXXXXXXXXXXXXXXXXXXXXXXXXXXXXXXXXXXXXXXXXXXXXXXXXXXXXX
XXXXXXXXXXXXXXXXXX.
                           *(1 space)*
XXXXXXXXXXXXXXXXXXXXXXXXXXXXXXXXXXXXXXXXXX?                *Body*
                           *(1 space)*
XXXXXXXXXXXXXXXXXXXXXXXXXXXXXXXXXXXXXXXXXXXXXXXXXXXXXXXXXXXXXXXXXXX
XXXXXXXXXXXXXXXXXXXXXXXXXXXXXXXXXXXXXXXXXXXXXXXXXXXXXXXXXXXXX
XXXXXXXXXXXXXXXXXXXXXXXXXXXXXXXXXXXXXXXXXXXXXXXXXXXXXXXXXXXXXXX
XXXXX.
                           *(1 space)*
XXXXXXXXXXXXXXXXXXXXXXXXXXXXXXXXXXXXXXXXXXXXXXXXXXXXXXXXXXXXXXXX
XXXXXXXXXXXXXXXXXXXXXXXXXXXXXXXXXXXXXXXXXXXXXX.
                           *(2 spaces)*          •
                                                 •
*Complimentary Close*                            Sincerely,
                           *(4 spaces)*          •
                                                 •
*Signature*                                      •
*Signature*                                      •
  *Identification*                               Gordon Burgett


GB:cc                         *IEC Block: Initials*
Encl.:annotated bibliography            *Enclosures*
cc:Somebody Else                        *Carbon Copies*

# Paper

The stationery commonly used for query and full cover letters is 8 1/2" by 11" white bond at least 20 weight or heavier. Avoid using onion skin paper or any other that claims to be erasable. Onion skin paper makes editors weep. It curls up after a few days of handling and later must be pinned down or held flat to be read. It also turns yellow. Erasable paper is simply too much of a good thing. Not only can your thumb erase every word if you're careless in its handling, so can anybody else's simply by touching it. If your typing falls short of perfection, use "liquid paper" or correction tape.

Shorter cover notes, such as those sent for newspaper travel submissions, are prepared on paper specifically trimmed to cover only the top section of the copy. This paper is 4 1/4" wide by 5 1/4" high. It has my name, address, and phone number printed at the top. See the example in Chapter 23.

# Letterhead

Do as you wish here. Many writing instructors urge students to rush to the nearest printer to purchase pounds of prepared paper, with matching envelopes, on the assumption, I presume, that if the paper looks impressive and weighty, your query letter will follow suit, and a go-ahead can't be far behind. (Which brings to mind the tale of the farmer who dressed his donkey in pinstripes to make him look like a man — but wound up instead creating two odd-looking asses!)

A query letter does what it aims to do when it provokes an editor into asking to see your manuscript. I'm not convinced that letterheads make much difference or that typing your return address connotes anything more than a return address.

Still, if you feel that a letterhead adds needed class to your presen-

tation, or shows more professional commitment, then make the investment. But do draw the line at identifying yourself as Tom Smith, Writer.
Or "Freelance Writer." Maybe because each time I see it the person
using such stationery can't write wrongs, and the self-proclaimed title
makes me laugh. A personal bias, of course. Yet a writer is one who
writes — and sells. A name, address, and phone number are sufficient
for a letterhead set in a type size and boldness consistent with a block
business letter and quiet enough not to detract from the body of the
letter. Letterheads are to identify and impress. If you use one, make
sure it does both. If you don't, you still have the body of the query to do
the impressing. The body is where the action is.

The same logic prevails for cover letters. What you say and what
you are selling will determine the outcome, if the letter itself isn't so
bizarre that it interferes. The one exception was noted in the last
segment: special paper for newspaper travel or short cover notes. And
that for expediency. When you're pumping out a dozen notes to
different newspaper editors at one time it gets mighty tedious having to
type your full address, etc., for each. Word processors make it easier.
But special paper is better yet.

# Heading

If you choose not to use a letterhead, the heading consists of your
return address, phone number, and the date, which follows the phone
number one or two spaces below. The separating space is optional.
With a letterhead, the date is centered below the printed letterhead.

Don't include your name with your return address, just the
number and street name, followed by the city, state (Post Office two-
letter abbreviations are preferred: CA, IL, NY, etc.), and zip code (not
separated from the state by a comma). The phone number includes the
area code, in parentheses. The date is the month written out, the day
the letter is written, comma, and the year. Write out street, city, and
month names.

# Inside Address

This is the name and position of the person to whom you are writing, the name of the publication or publishing house, the address, and the city, state, and zip code.

Why is this necessary since you are mailing the letter and the recipient surely knows who and what he or she is? One reason is that you want your query or cover letter to lead to future correspondence — when you send in your copy, when you query again after a successful sale, when they buy the reprint, and so on — and it is far easier for you to find this information from your copy of your letter than to have to look up the inside address again each time.

If the person has a title — Professor, Major, Reverend — spell it out, with the exception of Mr., Mrs., Ms, and Dr. If you are uncertain whether a woman is married, err on the side of Miss or cop out and use Ms (but without a period following it; it doesn't abbreviate any other word). With a position title (President, ABC Company; Dean, XYZ College; Secretary, Chamber of Commerce), list the title after the name if it fits conveniently. If not, devote a separate line to it, indenting that line if you are using the modified block form.

Don't use periods at the end of the lines in the inside address unless the last word is an abbreviation (Inc., Corp.). The spelling of the editor's name and the publication should be correct, of course. If you can't take the few seconds required to check both, how can the mis-named soul have much confidence in the factual accuracy of your query or the follow-up article? After all, you already missed the most important fact: the name of the person or firm that you expect to pay your bill!

# Salutation

Elsewhere we talk about finding the right recipient for your query letter. Let's assume, for now, that your letter should be sent to Mr. Greg Legg, Managing Editor, *Whippet Star*. Then your salutation would be

"Dear Mr. Legg:" Note the colon, as I just did in this sentence. Not a comma unless you and Greg are old legg-pulling buddies. (Also omit the quotation marks!)

Since query and cover letters are addressed to one person, should the recipient be unknown to you, don't resort to the aging stand-by, "Gentlemen:". A gentlewoman may well receive it — not so gently! Make yourself familiar with the publications you write. Find the proper name on the staff list in the last issue. Only as a last resort direct your letter to a title: "Editor," "Articles Editor," etc.

## Signature Block

This block consists of three chips: the complimentary close, the signature, and the signature identification.

The complimentary close is so indiscriminately used it has created a bias in my mind, to the degree that in my query and cover letters I seldom use one at all. Not that I don't want to be congenial or cordial in parting, which is its purpose, but because the standard choices are usually inappropriate and I can't think of a replacement that wouldn't draw undeserved attention.

For example, it is common for editors to wish you "best!" or "best wishes!" — often in rejection letters! Which is like praising your arrival while pushing you out the door. Yet if I wish them "best!" it sounds false.

"Yours truly" is hardly the case, except where it pertains to my copy in exchange for a healthy check. "Respectfully" isn't bad, but it would have a bit more sincerity if I knew them. "Cordially" may be the best of the lot. I'm not certain what "Regards" means in this context, and "Sincerely yours" is true to the point that there is sincerity in what the query or cover says and in my desire to write for the editor for a proper return.

How can I advise you, then, when I have struggled, mildly, with this social artifact, and lost? It may be unimportant which response you use, as long as it's not too bizarre. And it may not count a whit if you use one at all. I sometimes write my name large to fill the space below the text and above my typed signature identification, thinking that a missing complimentary close won't be noticed.

The signature presents no problem at all. Sign the letter in ink under the complimentary close or at a proper distance below the body flush left or along the imaginary vertical line. Don't use a rubber stamp or leave the space blank, unless your intent is to show that you consider the letter unimportant. Also, if your handwriting looks like you are a runaway from a mental ward, or were quietly diplomaed from the third grade, improve your scrawl. The only place on the query letter where your personal mark appears is at the signature. The rest of the letter could read as though it were written by the archangel of journalism but if your handwriting looks truly moronic, the editor may need just that excuse to say no.

Another thought: you may wish to use only part of your name or another name altogether. See the next chapter, about pseudonyms.

The signature identification should appear on the fourth line directly under the complimentary close, or under your written name. It tells who you are, typed so your scrawl can be identified. Don't use "Mr." Women may wish to indicate their marital status by writing (Mrs.) or (Miss) before their names, in parentheses.

There is seldom a reason to indicate your position or place of employment, much less to declare yourself a "writer" or "freelance writer." An exception would be if the topic of your proposed article would gain strength by such knowledge. A complex piece describing the newest techniques in brain surgery would be more quickly accepted if your degree, specialization, and institution were mentioned — if they were related to medicine! In such a case, unless these already appear in the letterhead or body of the letter, the degree follows the name. The section or department appear on the next line (if needed), and the company or institution, on the line that follows, all single-spaced and lined up under the first letter of the complimentary close.

## IEC Block

While an IEC block looks suspiciously like that clear stuff used on delivery trucks to keep milk cold when I was a kid, the letters actually stand for initials, enclosures, and carbon copies. Technically, they should be included as part of a proper business letter. In queries they seldom are.

The initials (GLB:cc, for example) indicate your name (first in upper case) and those of the person typing the letter (after the colon, in lower case). Yet most writers type their own query or cover letters, at least in the beginning, so this can be deleted. (Why fake it if you have no secretary? If the typing is bad, and you still send the letter, it shows poor judgment in keeping the secretary; if it's good, does the editor really care who does the labor?)

The enclosures might be anything from a manuscript to a $100 bribe for the editor to look at your prose. The first is what you are writing the query to avoid, by checking the sense of and need for the article. Logically it can't accompany the query. As for the $100, that would be better spent buying copies of this book for literate friends, or even passersby. In other words, unless they are other examples of your printed work with the query letter, which would surely be mentioned in the text, you are unlikely to have enclosures with queries.

Cover letters, on the other hand, accompany copy, so there the enclosures should be noted. Except with the short cover notes, like those sent to newspaper travel editors. They are stapled or attached directly to the copy and the paper they are typed on is so short, this formality can be overlooked.

Carbon copies. Of course you prepare a copy of the query or cover letter for yourself, but you needn't tell the editor that. You'd be thought foolish if you didn't. Who else would be interested, or even correctly included, in a business letter between you and editor? Only in those extremely rare cases where in fact a copy of that specific letter is sent elsewhere would you note it. That excludes simultaneous submissions cover notes. The fact that the material is being sent to others will either be noted on the manuscript itself, below the word count, or will be mentioned in the cover note itself.

In short, the IEC block probably doesn't appear a few lines below the signature on the margin, flush left, in most query letters because there is nothing to note. It is more likely to be used for cover letters. Our sample letter shows the location and order in which the items would be noted, if necessary.

# Body of the Letter

This is where the action takes place in query and cover letters. Nothing else should draw attention from it.

The body should be error-free, with wide margins and sufficient space at the top and bottom to look balanced. If you must continue on to a second page, be certain that at least a few lines of the text carry over, so that the signature block doesn't appear alone.

Some editors will refuse to read query or cover letters that can't be presented on one page, assuming that if you can't come to the point quickly in querying or selling printed text, the text itself will be as longwinded. One way to limit your letter to one page but offer more information than it will hold is to append attachments: an outline, an opening page of the manuscript, clippings or samples of previously printed work, a bibliographical guide, etc.

# 29

## Is a Pseudonym Ever in Order?

**N**ew writers sometimes choose to use a pseudonym, or pen name. Legally, that represents no problem unless it is done for fraudulent reasons. But it does have its inconveniences and it can raise doubts.

Try to deposit your check when it is written to the other you without endorsing the real you on the back, unless your account is under the pseudonym — which also has its difficulties.

Or have an editor try to find you when your real name and address or phone number are misplaced.

People you write about or work with may have the same difficulties. And interviewees sometimes feel uneasy working with a writer who doesn't use his or her own name, as if the use of a pseudonym absolves that writer of responsibility for what is written.

Perhaps the most important point to be made about pseudonyms is that whatever name you use, you are still legally responsible for what appears in print. And all assets under any of your names are available should legal action against you require some payment on your part.

## Reasons for Pseudonyms

Then why are pen names used? Novices usually take them for effect, though I fear they end up simply looking affected.

A more substantial reason finds a recognized writer in one genre also writing in another, and so not to confuse the public image, a different pen name is used in each. The publishers sometimes insist upon it. A well known children's writer who is also in print advocating the burning down of courtrooms and the stoning of judges will have two writing names!

The deacon of a church who moonlights in pornography would prefer to have a substitute, rather than baptized, name in boldface on the racks.

And at times, as we mentioned earlier in a different context, gender connotations may require slight — or total — name alterations, like our lass writing the hockey article for the boy's magazine. She either used her initials or picked out a more aggressive, masculine name.

## Why So Much Concern Over the Use of a Second Name?

A natural question that others will ask themselves, or you, is why a pseudonym is being used. Editors will be the first to wonder. There is always the thought that if the writer won't let his or her name stand with the research and writing, something must be wrong. Or that the same article is about to miraculously appear in another publication, and in a misguided attempt to escape the consequences of improperly selling the same copy twice, the writer has simply changed one authorship.

I'd certainly consider a pseudonym if my name had a foul or misleading connotation in English or in a foreign tongue into which I would be translated. (Fortunately, my surname means nothing internationally but what it says, and is equally as unknown, a fact surely to be rectified when this book hits the stands!)

You may also want to use a pseudonym if the article, when published, puts you or your family in undue danger, or if it compromises you in such a way that your using a different name would make sense to the editor. Explain your reasoning to that editor and request that your actual name be, as much as possible, confidential to the publication.

Use a pseudonym if you insist or it's clearly necessary, but be ready to explain why if that use suggests even the slightest touch of impropriety.

---

*"The first step in constructing a good query letter is to address it to the appropriate person. This sounds so obvious as to be almost ludicrous — but it isn't. There will be some instances which will be immediately apparent — e.g., fiction to the fiction editor or an article on banking to the financial editor — but in a great many cases you will be dealing in grey areas. A good rule of thumb is that the person at the very top of the masthead is not the one who assesses potential manuscripts and queries. Try the second or third person down the column in the editorial department or, better still, call the publication and ask for the name of the person you should address your query to.*

*"The second point is to be brief. State your idea as clearly and concisely as possible, then give a basic idea of what you intend to cover. It's better to be too brief than too wordy. If an editor's interest is piqued by your letter, he can contact you for further details. But if your letter doesn't hold his interest, he won't expect your article to. End your letter with a short review of your credentials as an author. If you have published before, say so and tell the editor where. If you haven't published but you have a particular expertise in the area you are writing about, explain that to the editor."*

Susan Carr Jenkins, Executive Editor, *Medical Times*

# 30

## Query Letters, Cover Letters, and the IRS

Y ou have one giant, pesky task if you are to properly deduct expenses from your income on Schedule C of your Form 1040 on or before April 15: you must convince the IRS, if asked, that your writing is a serious attempt to earn an income. That it's not a hobby.

You may know that and your spouse may know that too but without repeated sales, a reputation, and a recognized byline, your tax agent won't be so sure.

One way to guarantee acceptance of your deductions is to make a lot of money by writing. The very thing that beginners can't do because they are just getting started. So let's get that acceptance using two other tools: query letters and cover letters.

## Query Letters

Positive replies to query letters are "letters of intent." Ideally such a letter of intent would be a written response by the editor on the publication's stationery that says "I intend to consider, use, and pay you for your manuscript about ... "

Since that declaration of intention makes the preparation of the manuscript the completion of a business contract (even if the actual payment or amount is unmentioned), all reasonable costs incurred in its preparation are deductible. Those would include the paper on which it is written, the stamps and envelope in which it is sent, the typing tool needed for the legible manuscript preparation, the overhead, the costs of acquiring and preparing the information in the copy, and much more.

Unfortunately, editors rarely send letters of intent that even vaguely resemble the ideal. Most have probably never heard of the term. Instead they scribble on the top of your query "let's see it" and mail it back. Voila! That's enough! Any positive reply telling you to prepare the manuscript for serious consideration for publication is considered sufficient, I am told by the IRS.

And what if they don't buy it? You can still deduct all reasonable expenses incurred. The editor responded in good faith; you accepted and followed through on the contract in the same way. Editors generally won't buy until they see the final product: the idea, the words, the finished article. Thus you must produce the manuscript, as promised in the query.

Query letters are the professional's best friend. The written go-aheads are pure tax gold. (Oral go-aheads lack this verifiability. If an editor gives you an oral okay, ask that it be confirmed in writing for your tax records.)

## Query Letters Also Confirm Writing Volume

There is a second reason, virtually as strong, why query letters are a tax boon to writers at all levels.

If audited, you will be judged, in the hobby-business determination, by the volume of output you produce each year. If you send off a poem a month or jot a query every quarter, that doesn't speak strongly for your business claim. Too little too infrequently.

Keep a record of all items mailed and responses received. The number of items recorded or the volume displayed, and the potential income versus the actual costs claimed, will weigh heavily should the IRS attempt to disallow your claims because your writing is a hobby, where the costs are not deductible.

Query letters are the way professionals sell their skills. Keep a copy of each sent, plus every reply to prove that in fact the letters were received and responded to. Queries generate go-aheads, and sales generate reprints, rewrites, and other sales. From the volume professionally done and verified comes the right to deduct all reasonably related costs.

# Cover Letters

Cover letters figure heavily in the volume of potential sales. They are sales letters pure and simple. Instead of being sent to test the market's receptivity to an idea, and an article about it, they attempt to directly sell items already in existence.

Every cover letter sent, with each item it attempts to sell, should also be listed on your mailing record. The example below shows a simple way to keep track — and show the tax folk if they ask. Also, keep a copy of every cover letter, with the reply, to verify the volume actually mailed.

# Keep Records and Receipts

You will be making money by your writing, if you're not already. Keep a tally of all income: amount, date received, and what it is for. That's the fun part.

You must also keep accurate, verifiable records on all expenses. You must be able to prove how much money was spent, when, and how it related to writing if you want to take legal deductions.

If you pay with a check, mark in the lower left-hand corner what it is for. An example might be WRITING: STAMPS on a check to the Postmaster. Credit cards are acceptable too, if you keep the receipts and mark a similar notation on each. For individual receipts, also mark each and put it, with the rest, in a box or large envelope for tally at the end of the year. Finally, car costs (other than parking or toll receipts) are usually best claimed on the per-mile basis, so keep a booklet in your glove compartment in which you record, each time the car is used for writing-related purposes, the date, the mileage (or odometer readings), and how that relates to writing.

Examples of the last point. Your booklet might read:

May 12, 19 miles, interview with J. Hill for *Pet Life* interview
May 14, 3 miles, mail query letter
May 15, 26 miles, university library for research

# Keep a Mailing Record

As important as your receipts and records will be your mailing record, for agents will be as interested in how much money you could have made as how much you spent.

A simple but rigorously kept record will do. Mine notes the year and page number atop each sheet, with about six entries that are separated by an inch or two of space in which I can enter all that transpired relating to that query or submission.

Three entries on one page might read like this, to give you an idea:

May 15 - Q - Ozark banjo player     - *Music Journal*

May 16 -     Fee change at Yosemite          - *Chicago Tribune*

May 17 -     "Echolocation/whales" "Dolphin orientation"
                                                    - *Radar Reader*

A quick explanation of the above. In the first, the "Q" means a query letter. I'll record all that happens, by date, below it so I know what is taking place and, if necessary, so will Uncle Sam. The second is a simultaneous submission to newspaper travel editors; thus it is a manuscript being sent straight in. And the third is a reprint offer. Both articles have already been sold, so I'm offering second rights (also called reprint rights) to them to *Radar Reader*. The second and third items will be sent with cover letters, and I'll keep a note of all responses and follow-throughs in the space below the entries.

# The Disclaimer — and Encouragement

Alas, I'm not a tax expert and specific questions should be discussed with the IRS office, a tax accountant, or a lawyer.

But just keep querying and reselling. Keep clear records, copies, and receipts. Keep the faith and keep writing. And keep those deductions that are rightly yours. You earned them.

---

*"Appropriate query letters make an editor's job much easier, and enlightened self-interest is a powerful motivation.*

*"Above all, make sure your spelling, grammar, and punctuation are perfect. A well-written letter is the best writing sample you can present. A letter that is sloppily written or haphazardly typed (always type a query letter) will indicate to the editor that the manuscript would be just as sloppy — and possibly inaccurate."*

Susan Carr Jenkins, Executive Editor, *Medical Times*

# 31

# Some Words About Desperation — and Success

There are times when beginners are so damned mad about their inability to crack into what they see as the publishing "big time," they grow desperate. Anything can provoke that final break. A friend's negative comments or a spouse's indifference while reading your best work. A three-month delay ended by a mimeographed rejection. Despair creeps in and creates momentary madness.

In the grips of such *locura*, some writers drop to their literary knees and beg an editor to "give them a chance," to "let somebody, anybody, see their work," and so on. They plead that he or she is their last hope (an editor particularly likes to be offered a manuscript last!), and that unless their article is bought, they will quit writing — or worse. If there is a worse.

Sound like a pit into which you might stumble — or leap? Resist. It's simply too desperate, and too final: it assures defeat. What editor could ever rely on such an unstable writer? Would you put your riches in the hands of a person who came to your door begging and tearing out his hair and wailing that he just had to manage your money?

I have no cure for such desperation, simply advice against it — and compassion, for often I shared those feelings. Maturity includes patience and a reservoir of self-confidence. They are part of the toughness needed to succeed in freelancing.

There's another answer too, though one I offer with more than mild reluctance. Perhaps you should quit writing, at least for a while. Read, or take a few days off backpacking or looking up old friends or even talking to your mate. Restore some balance to your whole life. List all the things you do well and are sought for others. Soon enough you will be able to add writing to that list. Often that helps reduce the sense of endless rejection and eternal doom.

No panaceas, no magic cures. Just the certainty that there are ways to sell and ways guaranteed that you won't sell, and operating from a base of defeat assures the second result.

# And a Final Word About Success

Two writing friends made the same suggestion when reviewing this book in its final draft. They felt that the six preceding paragraphs were so depressing they should be left out.

Well, I overruled them because I knew that kind and depth of despair and I think all new writers experience it. I also kept the information in because I sincerely believe that if you can write at all and if you put the how-to aspects of this book to the test, you will see positive results soon — and desperation, rather than those paragraphs, will be cast out. (Mind you, despair is tenacious and will try to return. But well written queries and cover letters will chase it away as surely as garlic will put a vampire to flight!)

One thing is sure: professionals sell through the use of query and cover letters. This book tells you what those letters are, what they contain, when they are sent, who should receive them, and much, much more. You must find the idea and do the thinking, researching, sorting, writing, and editing. Together we can pull you through that hour glass to get your manuscript seriously considered and bought, then bought again and again. Enough buying and desperation will become a sad memory that you will be too busy to contemplate.

You are an important person, more so as a writer because you can share your uniqueness with many people. You put thoughts into words. You bring to others joy and hope and guidance and inspiration, laughter and thought and promise, and in the process you become a wiser person and a better writer.

Yet to be a writer in the complete sense you must be in print, and that requires an uncertain crossing of an indifferent and crowded sea. Query and cover letters are the vessels used by the "old salts." Jump abroad, and *bon voyage*!

# PART SIX

## Additional Query Letters, with Comments

## Query Example #4

123 Main Street
Carpinteria, CA 93013
(805) 123-4567
Month 1, Year

Mr. Ted Hanrahan
Editor, Newspaper Magazine
10 E. Barker Street
New York, NY 10000

Dear Mr. Hanrahan:

Two bets: (1) that your readers can't name three of the seven kings who ruled in the Americas, and (2) that they'd read an article about them, first word to last, if the piece were properly laced with humor, facts, and anecdotes.

Kings sell, particularly this lot: four were white, three black; some were home grown, others came from the oldest European lines; two couldn't read their names if they could write them, one translated Longfellow; one even killed himself with a silver bullet!

Who were they?  Three ruled the "gem of the Caribbean," the wealthiest colony in the New World during Napoleon's time: Haiti.  Jean-Jacques I (Dessalines) was a butcher of the worst blood yet the first to declare an American independence.  The statue in his honor in a Port-au-Prince park is the bust of a Central American despot!  Henry I (Christophe), a British free-boy sold into Haitian slavery who helped fight for U.S. independence, was Haiti's greatest king.  Faustin I came later.  He was picked from a hat, put it on his head, and ruled for 11 long, backward years.

Mexico's Augustin I (Iturbide) freed his country from Spanish occupancy, was deposed, and returned once too often.  He was no luckier against the firing squad than Maximilian a few decades later, who was summarily dispatched to a higher kingdom by Benito Juarez.  "Max's" wife went mad and a World War I battle in Belgium was moved a few miles away not to disturb her.

Pedro I, kin to Maximilian (who later fell madly in love with Pedro's tubercular daughter), was a wiry rascal raised in the royal Brazilian stables, issue of a mother unstable and a Portuguese king (Joao VI) on the lam from Napoleon.  Pedro I could master women and horses but couldn't harness his own will.  He left his five-year-old son to rule the hemisphere's largest land.  Pedro II grew to be 6'4", learned a dozen tongues, ruled for 49 years, and was responsible, in part, for the sudden fame of Alexander Graham Bell at the 1876 Philadelphia Centennial Exhibition.

I've been in print 350-plus times, and will gladly submit on speculation.  Are your readers ready for the royal treatment?

Thanks.

Gordon Burgett

# Query Example #4

# A General Interest Article for a Sunday Supplement

*Lead*

Selling a history piece is about as hard as selling an almost dead ox. Worse yet, the people being written about — kings! — aren't even from the United States. So this query letter has to read fast, well, and be particularly fetching. Even then, it is probably going to be rejected.

The idea of "two bets" is to pique the editor's curiosity. Can the editor, much less the readers, name three — or any — of the seven kings of the Americas? Does the editor even know there were kings in the Americas? And would that editor's subscribers read an article to find out more about them? I suggest that those readers will — if the piece is funny, accurate, and full of real-life accounts.

*Second Paragraph*

This paragraph might be eliminated, as I read it with hindsight. Its value is that it shows the variety of people discussed in the piece and, by implication, the breath of potential interest that variety might have to attract more readers. Kings sell, I tell the editor, as if I know and he doesn't! Black kings, white kings, local grown and imports, some educated, some as dumb as cactus, and just who was it who killed himself with that silver bullet? (Henry I)

*Body of
the Letter*

The next three paragraphs devote a sentence or two to
each ruler, capturing some humorous yet true facet of
his personality or fate, to draw the editor into wanting
to read more. It's crucial that these paragraphs read
well and the ideas flow, to keep the editor reading and
to show that the piece will be written in the same light,
tongue-in-cheek fashion. Wordplay is important too,
to convey the maximum of both meaning and humor
with a minimum of words.

*Conclusion*

How does the editor know that I had then been in print
in magazines 350 times? My word only. But the letter
looks and reads like it's written by a professional. I'm
not sure the editor cares, frankly. I'll submit on speculation. If the copy doesn't live up to the promise of this
query, the editor's not committed. But if I get a go-
ahead, I'll produce a top-grade article. Then if this
editor doesn't buy it, another will.

*Cost*

Three hours in the library, some facts picked up during
college studies, an hour with the *Writer's Market*
preparing a market list, and 20 minutes writing the
query.

*Time Factor*

The last king died over 100 years ago. The topic will
keep until the idea is sold many times in different
forms. No season is best here, making it an ideal general item for those magazines that print months in
advance.

*In Retrospect*

I'd redo the first and second paragraphs. The first, reading it years later, has a touch of defensiveness to it, a sort of daring the editor, of holding him or her to the wall and shouting a challenge. Or am I imagining that? The second adds little, as is. I'd rewrite it, with more exciting facts — or cut it out completely. The rest is okay. As it is, it worked.

# Query Example #5

123 Main Street<br>
Carpinteria, CA 93013<br>
(805) 123-4567<br>
Month 1, Year

Mr. Robert H. Rufa
Managing Editor, Travel
Floral Park, NY 11001

Dear Mr. Rufa:

> You got trouble, friend,
> Right here, I say,
> Trouble right here in River City!

River City exists! It's hiding in north-central Iowa much as Harold Hill described it in Meredith Willson's smash hit The Music Man.

The trouble, you recall, was the billiards hall, the Pleazol, and the path to salvation was a marching band, instruments bought sight unseen from the same Harold Hill.

If you go to Mason City today, walk north on Federal Avenue from Central Park and look down, you will see, in marble for all time: PLEAZOL! Alas, times change. The pool hall has moved four doors away. There's still trouble in River City!

I'd like to take Travel readers back to "River City" to see the source of so much fun. Seventy-six trombones still play to tapping feet somewhere in the world every night, 25 years after the musical made its debut!

We'll visit Meredith Willson's home town, walk the streets and talk with "plain men, modest men," then cross the bridge to see Marion the Librarian's old haunt (now housing Iowa Kempfer Mutual Insurance) or where Marion (Meredith's mother) lived, close to Willow Creek, the "river" of River City.

What's more, since Travel pieces include the surrounding area, we'll visit the Hobo Center of America, the "Little Brown Church in the Vale," the site where the 4H emblem originated, fossil beds throughout the region, a buffalo preserve, the only known habitat of a rare relict mouse, Hamlin Garland's home -- the kinds of places one finds in the country Midwest.

I've been in print 350 times, in travel, humor, and general interest. I'm not tooting my own horn, just Willson's flute as he did at the Cerro Gordo Hotel for the Kiwanis Club a Wednesday afternoon in 1912. That's how it all began for him and Mason City.

Interested? I can also provide "24 made-to-order 35mm slides as pretty as the American flag on the Fourth of July," as Harold Hill would say. A bit corny, but that's Iowa.

Gordon L. Burgett

# Query Example #5

# A Travel Article for a National Magazine

*Lead*

Instant identity is what your article's lead seeks, and if you can do the same in the query, great. In this case, since the proposal concerns *The Music Man,* the quickest way is to pluck lyrics from the musical. I will have to follow up that reference to trouble later.

*Second
Paragraph*

The focus of this piece is Mason City, the model for Willson's River City. And since the lead ends with "River City," the next paragraph picks right up on it. It exists. It's in Iowa. Much like it was described.

*Third
Paragraph*

Cite something that proves that Mason City still looks like River City. And bring in that trouble from the lead. What do you have? PLEAZOL, the pool hall.

*Fourth
Paragraph*

And there it is, in marble on the main street, PLEAZOL. By giving the precise location I show the editor that I have been there or at least have accurate, precise facts. I also took several photos of that word inscribed in marble, to add visual proof to the statement.

*Fifth
Paragraph*

At last, what I am offering: a chance for Rufa's readers to visit, in print, the source of the musical. In other words, an article! I also remind him that, despite the age of the musical, it is still very, very popular. That means his readers will still care about River-Mason City.

*Sixth
Paragraph*

A bit more about the town, to show that enough exists to merit an article and that I know enough to write about it.

*Seventh
Paragraph*

Here I show that I've at least read the *Writer's Market* write-up of *Travel's* needs, if not the magazine itself. The publication wants a focal point plus information about what its readers can do within a 50-mile radius. So I dig up additional facts to put more flesh on the map. A hobo center and a relict mouse aren't much, but I'm doing the best I can with what's available, folks. Just like you'll have to do. I could tell them that Disneyland is a few miles away, except that it's easier to prove the truth.

*Eighth
Paragraph*

I've worked my credits in, just in case the editor gets shaky with a beginner writing about the sticks. The chance to slip in more background about Willson and Mason City sets up the opportunity to sell my skills. The key thing is to keep centered on the topic and to bring it alive in one page.

## Conclusion

An action question: are you interested? And another chance to zip back to Harold Hill and Iowa while telling the editor that I have 24 good slides of the area.

## Form

This letter is long so I had to bend business letter convention. The complimentary close, which I seldom use anyway, was deleted to save space, keep the letter to one page, and to leave some white space to balance the presentation physically. I mention it only to emphasize, again, that nothing is sacred except the message.

## In Retrospect

This is one of my favorite query examples because it never strays from the topic. There's something else too.

By reading the query do you think I've already been to Mason City? Good, I want you think I'm on top of the subject. But I never said I'd been there, nor would that make much sense. I hadn't been close. Only the comment about the photos could be misleading — but I can provide them, after I take them when I visit the site!

The query's contents came from several hours of library work, phone calls to Mason City, reading a copy of the script, and a studying a map to list other interesting sites and features nearby. (The entire process forms the core of *How To Sell 75% of Your Freelance Writing*.) Add to the hustle a bit of common sense, some tight editing, and this query received a quick go-ahead, which in turn produced an article (with a cover photo) that ultimately repaid itself ten times over the original check.

# Query Examples #6-8

# The Same Subject Queried Simultaneously to Three National Publications

Article ideas are like fallen leaves, everywhere for the picking. Take the sunny morning of August 5, 1978, when I was parking my car before running in a 6.2-mile race in Ventura, California. A petite lass about 50 years old, in running shorts and a singlet, emerged from a VW in front of me and we exchanged "good day's" en route to the sign-up table.

Later, much to my surprise, I found myself racing the same tiny form to the finish line! On the way back to our cars we exchanged the usual runners' talk. She was extremely soft-spoken and modest. It was all I could do to find out how a grandmotherly waif could chug up and down hills and skim the beachfront at a sub-seven-minute-mile pace. The truth proddingly emerged: Margaret Miller, a Scottish transplant, wasn't an everyday jogger. She held both the American mile and world marathon records for women 50 and over!

That night I prepared a writing plan to sell articles about my newfound topic. I would phone *Runner's World* to confirm that she did hold both records, interview Margaret by phone to pick up the essential biographical facts needed for a query, read up a bit on women's long distance running to put their times and age into perspective, and then send query letters to an assortment of publishing markets.

Which markets would be interested in buying a story about a California grandmother who simultaneously held two of the most demanding running records? Surely a running magazine, and likely

# Query Example #6

123 Main Street
Carpinteria, CA 93013
(805) 123-4567
Month 1, 1985

Mr. Jon Larsen
Editor, The Runner
1 Park Avenue
New York, NY 10016

Dear Mr. Larsen:

Running's least likely record holder has to be 96-pound Margaret Miller, a 52-year-old Sears saleslady from Thousand Oaks, California.

For one thing, she is hypoglycemic and must follow a diet almost the reverse of her competitors. For another, until ten years ago the highlight of her life was being chosen a Highland Dancer in her home town of Glasgow, Scotland.

Now Margaret holds the world record in both the mile and the marathon -- for females 50 and over. Last week she set the distance record for her class for the one-hour run. When will it end?

I met Margaret when she parked in front of me at a 10K in Ventura, California, and later when we finished seconds apart. We shared some tea and words, and when I undiplomatically pried her age from her, I asked how many women her age could beat her. "None," she half-whispered, and the truth slowly emerged.

Must it emerge that slowly for The Runner's new readers? I'd like to share the "why's" of a 50-plus female who made a dramatic change in her life a decade back, and who will enter her first Boston Marathon this April, a lass who runs 55 miles a week between grandmothering, working, and nursing a running husband.

My writing background is on better footing than my own weekend running: 350 items in print -- tearsheets or copies gladly sent. Yet since I work on speculation, and sell better than 90% of that, what I need is a go-ahead, a copy of your new publication, and any length suggestion you wish to share.

Please let me know. Thanks.

Gordon L. Burgett

one from the women's market, a California publication (perhaps in-flight or regional), a retirement monthly, and perhaps some other, more general magazine.

*Runner's World* confirmed Miller's ranking, plus added another she held for her age: the one-hour distance record. Margaret turned out to be as warm and sharing during the phone interview as she was fast on the track. Even better, the preliminary interview yielded enough personal information to impart a sense of depth and intimacy to the query. Most important, she was flattered at the prospect of an article and showed every desire to cooperate with a fuller in-person interview and photographic session later.

Thus, with a $2 phone call to Mountain View and another $3.50 in calls to the Miller home, plus some hours in the library digesting the few tomes about female runners and records, I was ready to write one query that would serve as the base for other queries to non-competitive markets.

## Query Example #6: *The Runner*

Background

A new national running publication called *The Runner* was about to appear in New York. Since *Runner's World* had just printed a short bio about Carol Cart-wright, Miller's closest competitor (and subsequent record setter in the marathon), it was unlikely that they'd use material so similar again. So I aimed for the new magazine, uncertain of its format but counting on it to have a shortage of West Coast material at the outset.

*Salutation*

I saw Jon Larsen's name mentioned as the probable editor and knew that *New Times* (since folded), which he had edited, was published by the same house. So I mailed the query to him at the *New Times* address, and hoped.

*Body of
the Letter*

Larsen doesn't know Margaret Miller nor why he or his readers should, so my key task in the query is to flesh her out and make him want to know her better. Still, his readers are runners; their interests are running and other runners. Many are women; all are aging. Some (horrors!) are even approaching 50. So I emphasize the biographical facts that Margaret gave that make her both similar to the readers and still different: a Sears saleslady but from Scotland; 96 pounds, 52 years old, hypoglycemic (and why that matters to a runner); the world's fastest in her class; her modesty about her records yet her courage in entering the Boston Marathon; a grandmother who runs 55 miles a week, and so on ....

*Fourth
Paragraph*

Shows that I know her personally and won't be pasting together a second-hand rewrite, or worse. And that I run and am familiar with technical terms and jargon *The Runner*'s readers know, use, and expect to read.

*Conclusion*

Simply, I'm a professional and so confident that they will buy my copy I'm not asking for an advance and/or guarantee before I research and write. (Larsen doesn't know me anyway and likely wouldn't buy outright without seeing some evidence of my work.) I go a step further, saying that I'll submit on speculation so he can see that the work is the caliber he wants. He's got the cards. No time for bluffing. Just play your best hand, which is a good query followed by copy as good or better. It evens out later, when you've sold him some super articles.

## Query Example #7

123 Main Street
Carpinteria, CA 93013
(805) 123-4567
Month 1, Year

Mr. Richard B. Stolley
Editor, People Weekly
Time and Life Bldg.
Rockefeller Center
New York, NY 10020

Dear Mr. Stolley:

Margaret Miller is indeed likely to have been missed by one of your West Coast stringers. In fact I might not have found her either had we not all but literally crossed paths in Ventura, California, in a 6.2-mile race last Sunday!

Who is she? Margaret holds both the mile and marathon record -- for women 50 and over! Which, ten years back, would have shocked her neighbors in Thousand Oaks because the former Scottish Highland Dancer had never even run. Even today few of her co-workers at Sears know of this petite lass's long-run excellence. A grandmother at 52, Margaret wages a daily battle against hypoglycemia, and follows a diet so severe that she can't even "carbohydrate pack," which is the marathoner's way of storing energy for a long race. Instead, she sips cider, loosens her legs, and heads across the countryside, training at precisely 55 miles a week, and winning within minutes of her estimated goal.

In December, in San Pedro, California, she will attempt to better her own record for the third time. That might be an ideal date peg for publication, if the idea interests you.

My background includes 350 items in print -- tearsheets or copies of recent titles gladly sent.

Are you ready for a biography, a question-answer interview, or anything else about this latter-day 96-pound dynamo whose special kind of courage and joy sprung from utter despair only a decade back when, for more reasons than one, she began running for her life?

Please let me know. And thanks.

Gordon L. Burgett

Another point: I normally wouldn't query a magazine I hadn't read. If I did violate that rule, I certainly wouldn't let the queried editor know! But in this case *The Runner* wasn't even on the stands, so asking for a copy was proper. In fact, it was imperative, to see what it was printing, how it handled personality pieces, its article layout and lengths, the level and style of its photography, etc.

*Time Factor*

Projecting six months from the query date (to allow for manuscript preparation/pix and an estimated three-month lead time they need to work the material into the edition), we are in April, the month of the Boston Marathon. An ideal time release since Miller would be running in her first that same month.

*In Retrospect*

Somewhat choppy but it piqued the curiosity of the then Managing Editor, Marc Bloom: "Margaret Miller sounds like a fine subject for our People column — not only her running and all that entails but her dancing and other interesting aspects of her life."

## **Query Example #7:** *People Weekly*

Background

If you send the same query letter about the same idea to many publications at the same time, you could be faced with a lovely dilemma: they might all say yes!

First, you shouldn't send the same query to more than one. Each should be written to sell the idea to a different set of readers, and thus would require a different approach to the respective editors. True, many, even most, of the same facts would appear in the queries, but the promise, what each article would be about, must differ.

Second, you must write the letters in such a way that even if all the editors say yes, you can prepare manuscripts so clearly different that none can complain. In the manuscript just avoid using the same structure, similar leads or conclusions, identical quotes, and many of the same anecdotes.

Comparing the first query to *The Runner* about Margaret Miller with that of *People Weekly*, you will see the major changes in the first and fifth paragraphs, though there are subtle differences throughout. Let's review the *People Weekly* query item-by-item.

*Lead*

The then current *Writer's Market* indicated that *People Weekly* wanted subjects likely to be missed by its stringers. So the opening line restates that, adding that I too almost missed Margaret Miller.

*Second Paragraph*

Margaret who? This is where she must become human: why she should appear on his pages and why the readers would like to know more about her. Since the editor of a general magazine probably knows less about running than the editor of *The Runner*, I explain in greater detail what hypoglycemia means to a marathoner, and what carbohydrate packing is. You will notice that in this letter and the next a 10-K race becomes a 6.2-mile race.

*Third Paragraph*

*People Weekly* is just that, a weekly, so it needs date pegs, reasons for things appearing when they do. Here I give one: In December, Margaret will once again attempt to better her record.

*Fourth
Paragraph*

In the *Writer's Market* of that year *People Weekly* requested biographies, question-answer interviews, and shorts, so I suggest that "this latter-day 96-pound dynamo" might be the subject of any of the three.

*Conclusion*

I like to end queries with some spur to action on the editor's part, at least to let him or her know what I expect. "Please let me know" is a modest request. Finally, despite what business letter writers say, it never hurts to thank people, or so my mother told me. Thanks, Mom.

*If both
publications
say yes?*

I would focus heavily on the running, records, and times, with Margaret's other virtues woven in, for *The Runner*, and concentrate on the "whole Margaret" for the general piece in *People Weekly*. The leads, pix, quotes, conclusions, and anecdotes would be different. Which means more work for me. More interviewing, more quotes, more facts — and two checks.

*In Retrospect*

I might not have told enough about Margaret. Perhaps another paragraph or two, with some quotes or an anecdote, would have brought her more alive. That might have stretched the query to two pages, which has drawbacks. Who knows? You do what you can to get the sale. If you get a go-ahead in one of the three, great. Probably closer to 1:7 in the beginning.

## Query Example #8

123 Main Street
Carpinteria, CA 93013
(805) 123-4567
Month 1, 1985


Mr. James Wiggins
Executive Editor,
    Dynamic Years
215 Long Beach Blvd.
Long Beach, CA 90802


Dear Mr. Wiggins:

Having taken on and conquered the gray whales, I have an even more exciting story for you: the gray marathoners!

The center of my query is a former Highland Dancer turned world record holder in both the marathon and the mile -- for women 50 and over. Margaret Miller is a 52-year-old Sears saleslady, grandmother, and hypoglycemiac of Thousand Oaks whose 96-pound frame was as far from athletic excellence ten years back as her mind was from happiness.

How she brought her life into balance and went on to set a handful of world running records might be the focus. Or Margaret as one of the emerging matrons of the long run, with the focus on the 50-plus runners in the world today, male and female.

There are two time factors worth considering. In December she will attempt to better her marathon record for the third time, in San Pedro. And next April she will enter her first Boston Marathon, if injuries don't interfere. The Boston event might be a particularly good publication target, allowing me to expand the piece to include other older runners who will be competing in running's most prestigious distance race.

We first met while competing in a 6.2-miler in Ventura, running side-by-side the entire way! We've spoken for hours since, I've made the usual cross-checks for truth, and what has emerged is a story any reader would enjoy, full of spunk, laughter, courage, and a special kind of joy from a lass who turned to running in sheer despair.

Are we to team up again to delight your readers?

Thanks.


Gordon L. Burgett

# Query Example #8: *Dynamic Years*

*Background*

The more queries you write about the same subject, the more important it is that you change the focus of the proposed article. The third query, to *Dynamic Years*, suggests three possible ideas and two target dates. Yet it is the readership of *Dynamic Years* which provides the unique approach of its contents: they are the first post-50 group anticipating or already enjoying retirement.

*Lead*

I had just sold them an article about whales, and I like to follow up a sale with a query soon afterward, so my name stays fresh. I mention the whales in the query's lead and tie it to marathoning.

*Second Paragraph*

Nothing new here. Same facts from the other queries except that I bunch together her age category, her age, and that she is a grandmother, all near the top of the query because these are of particular interest to *Dynamic Years*.

*Third Paragraph*

I suggest two approaches or slants to the topic: Margaret herself or Margaret as one of the many 50-plus runners of both sexes in the world today.

*Fourth*
*Paragraph*

Time factors are included, plus another slant. If he needs the piece soon, the December record, if broken, might be included. But if he wants to wait, she might be more newsworthy, and the photos broader in subject, if prepared after the Boston Marathon. That adds another angle: the older runners at the Boston.

*Fifth*
*Paragraph*

We teamed up before, I remind him, so why not again?

*In Retrospect*

Not bad. Might say more about Margaret.

*If all three*
*say yes?*

Back up the money truck.

## Query Example #9

123 Main Street
Carpinteria, CA 93013
(805) 123-4567
Month 1, 1985

Juvenile Editor
Random House, Inc.
201 E. 50th St.
New York, NY 10022

Dear Juvenile Editor:

Chewing gum in the stacks of America's libraries?  Bubble Delight oozing from every page of a book?  A librarian's curse -- unless it's from Random House's fun, fact-filled cartoon/copy book about the history of gum called The Chicle Kid.

No, I haven't got my tongue in my cheek.  It's that much maligned substance first introduced into the United States by the victor of the Alamo, a former President of Mexico who was trying to earn his way back home by hawking a rubber substitute.  Worse yet, the first man to sell gum in volume was a dentist!  Cavemen chewed it, Mayans made rain shoes from it, and girls popularized it as a substitute for "chawin' tobacker."  By the end of World War II it was the best known currency on the globe.

Enclosed are the first ten pages of the total 48, with cartoons drawn by Larry Litsinger.  The prose and illustrations are offered together or separately.

Two of my degrees are in history.  More than 350 of my writings have appeared in print.  And I was in the sixth grade, with seven cavities, before I became, to avoid parental persecution, a close-lipped chewer.

If the sample sets your mouth to watering, let me know quickly: the rest of the tome will be in the next mail.  The Chicle Kid is eager to make some publisher rich.  He's chomping at the bit.

Is Random House ready to bite off something it can chew with a smile?

Thanks.

Gordon Burgett

# Query Example #9

# A Juvenile Book for a Publisher

*Attachment*

Ten pages of the 48-page juvenile booklet accompanied the letter, so the reason for and composition of the query in this case changes considerably. When a query is sent alone, the editor judges you by its content and composition, unless that editor knows you from an earlier contact. In this case, the query is as much a cover letter, and is less important as a sole selling tool. The first item of consideration will be the actual copy, the sample pages of the booklet. Only a letter in astonishingly bad taste or one that raises serious doubts about your authorship of the copy would dampen the editor's enthusiasm to see more of a good book.

*Lead*

Having said the above, it would seem prudent to write a three-line cover note simply telling the editor what is being sent, what I am selling (prose and illustrations together or separately), and what I have waiting to send, if the editor is interested. I can't argue with that logic; it might sell. And if the editor is close-lipped about more than gum chewing -- that is, if he or she has no sense of humor — indeed this lead may get the project set aside before it's ever really considered.

Yet the booklet is funny and the cartoons, funnier. A somber editor won't buy it anyway. So the letter may show that I can write humorously in more than gum books, and it should at least hint at items in other sections of the book that the editor doesn't have in hand, as well as contain the one-paragraph mini-biography. Since this is as much a cover letter as a query, it must be short. So why not fun, fact-filled, and to the point, like the booklet?

Who shudders most at the thought of chewing gum? Librarians, school teachers, and dentists. So we play on the fears of the librarians in the lead. Publishers are particularly aware of librarians: they buy books. We face that concern, straight on and with humor, that the librarian may reject a book about gum.

Mentioning the company receiving your query in the lead isn't a bad idea either. Since I don't have a name of a specific editor, tying in the company personalizes the letter a bit. It can't hurt to wed your book with their name, lovingly.

*Second Paragraph*

The history of gum? Why not highlight a few facts and humorous oddities to remind the editor that even gum can have a history sufficiently noble to have been jawed about since people hid in caves?

*Third Paragraph*

Business, quick and plain. The editor may want every book bought to contain at least 66 pages — or 366. There's a risk in noting that the book is 48 pages long. Yet a clever editor will discover its length soon enough anyway, and by stating it you now have a basis for dickering. It can be stretched to 66! (But 366?) It's also important that the editor know that you aren't the illustrator's Siamese twin, that the copy and the cartoons can be bought separately or together.

*Fourth*
*Paragraph*

The simplest of biographies — of me. I wrote the prose, I'm selling the book. The editor will likely have a house artist for illustrations. If Larry's work is nonetheless chosen, great; I'll fill him in later. In three sentences the editor knows that I have more than two degrees (can probably read and write), two are in history (so I might be able to tell a fact from a fiction), I've managed to bribe or woo at least 350 other editors to put an item of mine in print (either expect a bribe or good writing), and that at least in the sixth grade, when I had teeth, I had first-hand experience with the substance in question.

*Conclusion*

More of the same malarky — but not madness. If you want more, I say, I'll send you the rest. It's done and ready to go. Not a tease. The book has been written and illustrated; you can see it in a week. And I think it will make somebody money, besides me.

*In Retrospect*

It's a good query-cover, fast and to the point, setting the editor up humorously to leap into the hilarity of the booklet. Even if the editor printed a gum book last week and swore on a stack of copyright forms to resist such sticky matters forever, the letter says "writer" and "humorist." Maybe that editor has been waiting for just that combination to turn out the definitive work on armadillos. The query shows me to be the ideal person to pen that specialty. After all, if I can write about gum.... So instead of replying to me "no, get lost," the reply may be "no, not this time, but you might be interested in..." I'd have to be terribly hard-shelled to refuse.

# Query Example #10

123 Main Street
Carpinteria, CA 93013
(805) 123-4567
Month 1, 1985

Ms Tanya Wright
Articles Editor, Fun Abroad
88 West 33rd. St.
New York, NY 10000

Dear Ms Wright:

In mid-December I will again be headed for England and Wales, and would like to prepare two articles for you when I return.

The first, for use a year hence in your holiday or December issue, would be "Seeing London For Christmas." I could have it to you, with slides or b/w prints, any time after February 1, should that deadline be particularly early.

London is truly lovely for the holidays -- but people must know where to go and how to apportion their time. For one thing, three holidays in a week (Christmas, Boxing Day, and New Years), make museum visiting and sightseeing difficult, and shopping hectic and spotty. To offset that, it's easier to get theater tickets, parties abound, pubs hum with excitement, and many tourist sites do remain open, to be enjoyed casually without the crowds. Plus an added attraction then: trains uncrowded to Dover, the Hovercraft to Boulogne, and a wonderful day (or several) in France.

It is precisely that which I'd research this winter, to prepare the best action guide for the year to come, taking photos now and updating the details, if you wish, next fall right before final print time. Full of visuals, quotes, anec-dotes, some seasonal lore of England, and -- most important -- accuracy.

The second piece might be for use in the summer. It might be called "The Beaches of Wales," where much of England enjoys its holidays. Wales is a land of castles, pubs with song, choruses, forts, forests, pride, inns. And the visiting English, who in themselves are a delight to see and hear.

I was there last summer, briefly, but will return this winter for ten days to complete the research and supplement, if nature permits, some shots of the castles. In the process I hope to add to my store of interesting facts and insights, on what's "best" to see and do, where to stay, and when one should make reservations. Thus it could be a summer story, as suggested, or a March piece about "summering in Wales." The choice is yours. I could have the copy and pix in your hands by January 20.

For years I wrote travel in the Midwest, with some 200 articles in print and twice as many newspaper items. In the past few years I've tried to visit Europe annually, and have usually touched London and Wales each time. I'd like to share the loveliness of each with those seeking beauty and Fun Abroad.

Please let me know in the SASE soon so I can make my on-site plans accordingly.

Gordon Burgett

# Query Example #10

# Pre-Trip Travel Query Letter

*Lead*

This says it all: I'm going on a trip and want to know if I should gather information there for later stories for your readers. It tells when and where. Your query can be sent as early as six months before the trip.

*Second Paragraph*

Now you tell the editor when you will be back, by implication here (early or mid-January, to give yourself time to write good copy and get the photos developed), and, more important, when the copy will be in her hands. Since many magazines prepare their Christmas or holiday issue as early as March the preceding year, this shows professional savvy. The worst the editor can say, other than "no," is that she doesn't need it until later.

*Third Paragraph*

Here you show why the trip this year will produce a super article for the following Christmas. It sounds like you know London and are particularly conscientious about accuracy — a festidiousness editors love. There's plenty of spunk and fun promised too.

*Fourth
Paragraph*

More of the same. Good to note that you'll update the facts later. A quick call to the British travel board, in the U.S. if you have a few days, in London if not, will get the details adjusted.

*Fifth
Paragraph*

I generally limit each query to one idea, to give it a full-page sales treatment, but here, as you see, is an exception. As long as I'll be there and wanting to see Wales, why not ask for a go-ahead on a beach piece?

*Sixth
Paragraph*

You'll note that the paragraphs in my query are short, much as my copy will be, rarely more than three sentences long, usually one or two. Show by example how the writing can be expected to look.

Here I zero in on one story but from two different angles: it's all a beach piece, but either to be run during the summer or in the spring about the summer, so those wanting to visit those same Welsh beaches will have time to make arrangements. I let the editor tell me which, and promise a quick manuscript if she will use it in the spring. I don't ask if she wants an article, but which. An ancient salesman's trick, but I am selling, aren't I? And what a prize she'll win if she says "yes": electric prose, radiant verbs, azure nouns, joy with a splash!

*Seventh
Paragraph*

A bit about my background — and why I am the person to cover London and Wales.

*Eighth
Paragraph*

A simple request which gently reminds Ms Wright that I will be doing the work for someone and I must know for whom and which readers before I leave.

*In Retrospect*

Somewhat skimpy on the details about both articles, which confirms my prejudice against trying to squeeze two queries onto one page. Yet it may work. Both are legitimate topics — London off-season, and Wales, off the track. And it makes sense to do the legwork for both at the same time. Unless she knows that London at Christmas is wet and drab and the beaches in Wales feel like a drizzly tundra come January. If she gives me the go-ahead, I'll put on the union suit and get the facts. The readers will be none the wiser!

# PART SEVEN

## Additional Cover Letters, with Comments

## Cover Example #3

GORDON BURGETT
123 Main Street
Carpinteria, CA 93013
(805) 123-4567

Dear Mr. Rosenberg:

"The Land of The Music Man" is a tree-lined Main Street in Iowa called Mason City where Meredith Willson grew up, was raised by "Marion the Librarian," played pool at Pleazol (with its name still in marble on the sidewalk), and used a bridge to go to school that was later immortalized by the musical/movie. The article attached tells what the Washingtonians would find today, unchanged, in the setting should they head west for a visit....

I have 36 good-to-excellent b/w's available to select from, if interested -- or I can send the five best.

Please don't return the ms, just your verdict in the SASE. Thanks.

Gordon Burgett

# Cover Letter Example #3

# Simultaneous Submission Cover Letter

*Purpose*

This cover note will be read by the editor, enchant him, draw his eyes to the first paragraph of the copy, and let that pull them through to the last throbbing word on page six, eight, or whatever. Therefore it is stapled prominently on the upper left-hand corner on the front of the first page. Other copies of the same manuscript are being sent to other newspapers that do not overlap in circulation, each with its own note.

*Form*

See that the return address includes my phone number, on the long shot that the editor wants to call me to arrange a million-dollar deal. Or get the photos pronto. The note is short, quick, outlines the article in the first paragraph, talks of photos in the second, begs a verdict in the third, and lets those eager eyes dance to my magnetic wordplay on the manuscript.

*Attention*

This is sent to the editor of *The Washington Post* so it talks about Washingtonians and of going west to reach Iowa. Change the tie-in's in each note or you'll have the travel editor of the *L.A. Times* with the wrong name and heading to China to reach Mason City!

*In Retrospect*

It was one of my most successful travel submissions, and this note didn't hurt. It makes you want to read more. Just enough tease to do the trick. But then you have to have a good manuscript attached. Nobody, not even the most desperate editor, buys these little notes! But a lot will read the manuscripts if the notes pique their interest, and that, folks, is what it's all about.

*Another Point*

You have read about Mason City already. In an earlier query letter to *Travel Magazine* you saw this idea first being offered for print. By the time this note was written the magazine article had appeared and two reprints had already been sold. The same material has again been rewritten, in a shorter version, and is now being offered to newspaper travel editors.

# Cover Example #4

123 Main Street
Carpinteria, CA 93013
(805) 123-4567
Month 1, Year

Ms Thelma Schooler
Managing Editor, Women's Reader
1683 Wilbraham Ave.
Lynchburg, VA 20000

Dear Ms Schooler:

"River City, U.S.A.," the setting of Meredith Willson's beloved musical, The Music Man, could be anywhere the audience imagined, from Virginia to Montana. It was a mythical place of marching bands, Harold Hill, Marion the Librarian, and all the nostalgia of 1912 as vibrant and young as home-stirred ice cream on the Fourth of July!

But do your readers know that there really was a River City? And many of the places they've woven into fantasy really exist, like Pleazol, the pool hall, and the bridge over the river where the movie band marched and played "Seventy Six Trombones," and the library and the city park?

Where is "River City" and what's it like? That's the article I'd like to share with your Women's Readers -- the city itself, what visitors to it can see of the musical and Meredith's life there, what the residents think of their fame (or is it notoriety?), and how your readers could enjoy, in person, what we can first let them enjoy on paper.

It's really Mason City, Iowa, as the article attached, from Travel Magazine, reveals. They purchased first rights and used the piece in July, 1974. I'm offering you second rights, Ms Schooler, plus an assortment of 40 35mm slides (as well as the shots you see in the article) for illustrative selection.

I'll gladly add any of three sidebars to bring the story more directly to your readership: (1) a detailed list of events in and near Mason City the month, and the following two, that you plan to use the piece; (2) an interview with Mrs. Adele Lindune, the last of Meredith Willson's teachers still living, with humorous recollections of him and the town, and/or (3) a collection of interviews from women on how the town has changed because of the movie and musical.

If the article (and sidebars -- indicate which) interest you, I'll gladly send the original manuscript, the new sidebars, and as many slides as you wish to review. Simply let me know in the enclosed SASE.

The Music Man is America's favorite. Although I've been in print 400 times, the enclosed article shows all. If we can team up to delight your readers, great!

Gordon L. Burgett

# Cover Letter Example #4

# Reprint Simultaneous Submission Letter for a Travel Article

*Purpose*

Earlier in this book we read a query letter offering to write an article about Mason City, site of "River City, U.S.A." in *The Music Man*. At this point that query received a go-ahead, the article was written, and it appeared in *Travel Magazine*, which bought first rights. So we are writing a letter (one of many like it, each adjusted to its respective publication) to see if, here, *Women's Reader* would be interested in using the very same piece, or a modification, as a reprint.

*Lead*

Thelma Schooler has never been approached about this piece before, so we must sell her in the opening.

*Second Paragraph*

More of the same: what's this letter, with attachment, all about? It's harder to sell a reprint, so this cover letter needs all the care you'd put into a query.

*Third Paragraph*

Now we tie it to why the *Women's Reader* would be interested, though in truth it is a general article no more directed to women than men.

*Fourth*
*Paragraph*

Our legal obligations: I'm offering a reprint (as if Ms Schooler couldn't guess from the article copy enclosed!), where it appeared first, when, what rights they bought, and what else I have to sweeten the deal. Slides!

*Fifth*
*Paragraph*

Thelma's thinking to herself, why do I want to use that old piece everybody has already read? So here I suggest three ways that we can put a new dress on a known body, two of them women-oriented! On the other hand, she may think her readers have never seen *Travel* and would like to use the original unadorned. So I give her four choices, plus photos. Her lucky day!

*Sixth*
*Paragraph*

Two things here. One, let me know if she's interested. Two, Thelma may be of saintly stock but I want to keep tabs on her if she is thinking of using my prose *gratis*. Her typesetter will want it double-spaced (like the original manuscript), so I offer to send that to her, if interested. If she requests it, I will watch future *Women's Readers*. My gilded words see print, I see flakes of that gold.

*Finale*

Why any editor would buy this piece: it's about America's favorite musical and I wrote it! Be positive but not oppressive. At least don't be negative — and convincing!

# Cover Example #5

123 Main Street
Carpinteria, CA 93013
(805) 123-4567
Month 1, Year

Dr. Albert Seekins
Editor, Marathoner World
654 Fifth Avenue
New York, NY 10000

Dear Dr. Seekins:

The "Three-Peak Marathon" falls about 26 miles short of the mass appeal of the Boston or the Big Apple. It's nowhere near as tough as the Pike's Peak horror nor as grueling as the Western 100. But it has its own cruel sort of charm any true marathoner would love!

For one thing it covers some of America's loveliest terrain, though it's seen either climbing or descending. The race leaves Ojai, setting of "The Six Million Dollar Man" and the earlier film site for "Shangrai-Lai," up a six-mile, 1300' ascent past Lake Casitas, where the last Olympic rowing was held.

Eight miles down to sea level, past lemon and avocado groves along a twisting mountain road, leads the runners to a seemingly vertical 1.3-mile rise to the peak of Shepherd's Mesa, which the runners circle in a sea-view eerie of pastoral calm, in sight of Jose Ferrer's ranch, and back down to sea level. Too soon, at 23.5 miles, the last test of the true runner's dedication comes in the form of a steep .7-mile rise, past Dame Judith Anderson's former mansion, to the idyllic groves of Cate School. From then on it's downhill to the California coastal town of Carpinteria, a few miles south of President Reagan's summer White House.

Why would any sane human undertake this vertical torture? And why in backlands California far from the baddening crowds? The enclosed article tells all, as it did to the readers of Coastal Trails in January of this year. I'm offering reprint rights to your readership, 99% of whom likely live outside the other magazine's circulation.

I also have available a wide assortment of top-quality slides and b/w prints of the past three marathons, all held on cool, sunny days. Let me know your preference and I'll send you a choice of the best.

Finally, it's hard to set copy against a clipping like that enclosed. If you'd like the original manuscript, for your typesetter's peace of mind if not eyesight, just let me know.

The "Three Peak Marathon" is held in January when much of the rest of America is knee deep in snow so it makes ideal mid-winter copy. I can update the piece to include any details about the coming event (and notables scheduled to run) if used before the race, or I can give an account of the next actual run, if used after.

It's not the big time but it's one of the toughest, and surely among the loveliest, races anywhere in America. Something drew back 62% of last year's participants for a second time! In fact it's the best of both worlds: excrutiatingly delightful!

Should we share it with the readers of Marathoner World?

Gordon Burgett

# Cover Letter Example #5

# Reprint Simultaneous Submission Letter for a Sports Article

*Purpose*

Covers different ground in almost the same way the previous reprint letter did, so let me zero in on the few novelties in this write-up. Yet the purpose is identical: to sell an article again that has already been shared with the general public, in this case about a mythical marathon over actual terrain in a supposed running journal called *Coastal Trails*.

*Paragraphs 1-3*

Telling why *Marathon World* needs this article, with as much legitimate scene painting and name dropping as possible. I'm certain that a runner scaling Shepherd's Mesa after topping the peaks from Ojai could care less if a home along the route is owned by Judith Anderson or a hobo, frankly. But it makes an appealing visual in the letter — and is true.

*Fourth Paragraph*

The legal obligation again. Plus the fact that almost none of the *Marathon World* readers read *Coastal Trails*, which is important to Dr. Seekins.

*The Rest*

Three things make the piece more appealing: (1) it is run in the dead of winter, when live race copy is hard to find; (2) I can write it before the race, highlighting the event to come (with details about it) but focussing on facts and photos of past runs, or (3) I can zip material about the actual run as quickly as I catch my breath and get the words on paper. The last two offer a different manuscript than that already in print.

*In Retrospect*

It might just be the off-beat, out-of-the-norm piece that a large running publication will use, even as a reprint. Since it already made money as a sale, what have I — or you — got to lose trying to build on it again and again?

## Cover Example #6

123 Main Street
Carpinteria, CA 93013
(805) 123-4567
Month 1, 1985

Mr. Greg Kelsey
Editor, World News Syndication
4444 Fifth Avenue
New York, NY 10000

Dear Mr. Kelsey:

The three articles enclosed, about the Amazon, should find interested readers abroad, thus I am sending them to you for placement outside North America. (I am still selling reprints of all three in the U.S. and Canada, however.)

The first, "Gold in the Oriente!," is a first-person adventure piece of a gold hunt I led up the headwaters of the Amazon, the Napo, in remote Ecuador. From the Napo eight of us, all but one Vietnam War veterans, pushed and poled a 3500-pound dugout six days up the Paushi-Yaco and Chapano Rivers, through the Auca Indian territory, into an aquatic land never seen by outsiders. What we found and how we survived are the heart of the 2500-word piece that has already been in print five times in the U.S. Three sample slides, with captions, of 50 available, show how the excitement and danger are brought alive on the page.

The second, "The Jungle Opera House," is centered on the famed Manaus opera house, 1000 miles up the Amazon, being gutted and rebuilt, true to the original in every detail -- except that the new house will have restrooms for the audience and performers! I was given three hours to roam inside, camera in hand, to record the rebuilding. To that I have added the lore, laughs, and location of a cultural monument in one of the world's wildest cities. Sample slides enclosed, with captions, of 60 available for choice.

And the third, "Rafting on the Ocean Sea," is an adventure I stumbled into, a trip 20 miles into the Atlantic Ocean from Salinopolis, Brazil, near the mouth of the Amazon, on a flat raft, a _jangada_ like those brought with the slaves from Africa in the 1500's. The purpose? To catch marlin! The problem, though, is that sharks cruise a few feet away, you are usually ankle-deep in water as waves bathe the deck, and how do you keep from slipping off? The article, and slides, tell all! Three slide samples, with captions, from 60 choices.

If any or all of these interest you for sale abroad, just let me know and I will send more slides (indicate the number) for your selection.

I also have material, three articles each, about Iceland and England. Interested?

Gordon Burgett

# Cover Letter Example #6

# Syndication Cover Letter

*Purpose*

This letter combines elements of both cover and query letters. It is a cover letter since it accompanies actual manuscripts and offers them for reprint. The last paragraph has a query pitch in it, though syndication letters are as often as much soliciting interest in a future trip or article as they are trying to sell material in unused markets.

*First Paragraph*

Right to the point: Amazon stories for sale outside North America because I am still working that market. No reason to dance about with syndicates. Tell them what you have and what you propose, so they can dispose.

*Paragraphs 2-4*

Three paragraphs, three articles: you get a few sentences to bring each offering alive. Since you're sending copies of the articles with this letter, these sentences should make the editor want to read each. Focus on what makes the pieces unique and interesting and why they should be bought from you — now.

*Photos*

In this case I am sending three sample slides, with captions, of each story, with an indication of what else I can send later, if interested. Naturally I've picked nine top slides. Teasers. Sometimes syndicates will sell just the slides, but that's extremely rare. Without photography of some sort, if the piece is travel-related, it will seldom be bought.

*In Retrospect*

This is the lazy way to sell overseas, and it is only mildly effective. Letters like these work well within this framework, although you can do a page apiece about each article. I'm not sure the extra time and writing is justified in terms of the extra sales, though. If an editor can't be coaxed in a paragraph to read what's at hand, a page won't likely do any better.

## Cover Example #7

123 Main Street
Carpinteria, CA 93013
(805) 123-4567
Month 1, 1985

Ms Katie Sara Muldoon
Filler Editor, Nautical News
888 Sea Lane
Baleia, Maine 00100

Dear Ms Muldoon:

There's seldom a reason to send a cover letter with a filler, but I thought it prudent to explain how I know that some of the world's best known sea folk suffered badly and often from seasickness.

Prince Henry the Navigator, reputed father of oceanic exploration through his "school" at Sagres, in Portugal, went to the sea once and nevermore. This fact appears in three writings of the time, one original and two copies that I reviewed in the Greenleaf Collection in Chicago. (I read Portuguese fluently.) In one text he describes the effects of seasickness and says that is why his voyages were on paper, not on board.

Admiral Nelson, of the British fleet, complained regularly in his memoirs of his weak stomach and the despair he faced each time the anchor was lifted, calling his "sea sickness" a test of his love for his country.

And John Paul Jones, like Nelson, considered it the cost of a naval life, and spoke of it regularly, from which it passed into reputable history texts.

I'll gladly provide the tomes, pages, and citations, if you wish, but felt it best to simply set your mind at ease that though the filler seems contrary to fact, it is only contrary to what most imagine. Which is what makes it an interesting filler!

Respectfully,

Gordon Burgett

# Cover Letter Example #7

# Filler Cover Letter

*Purpose*

Sometimes fillers seem contrary to fact and it makes sense to set the editor's mind at rest with a short (or even long) note to reassure, in this case Ms Muldoon, that your items are based on something more than contrariness and/or wishful thinking.

So here we tell how we know about Prince Henry, Admiral Nelson, and John Paul Jones. Even better, cite the most reliable source or two in each case.

Alas, the seasickness of Prince Henry and Admiral Nelson is true and easily proved, but I made it up for John Paul Jones, just to give you an example! I couldn't stoop to providing that third source, have it fictional, and have some poor soul spend months scouring stacks looking for it for a master's thesis. Even cover letter writers have scruples. (Fortunately scruples aren't as bad as seasickness!)

Incidentally, I could have added, to those with motion sickness (of which seasickness is a liquid variety) Lawrence of Arabia, who was afflicted on camels, and one of my daughters, in a car. But why would the readers of *Nautical News* cared?

# Cover Example #8

123 Main Street
Carpinteria, CA 93013
(805) 123-4567
Month 1, 1985

Mr. Ron Damron
Managing Editor, The Sightseer
775 Wabash Avenue
Chicago, IL 60000

Dear Mr. Damron:

The enclosed article, about Providencia, the Caribbean island near Nicaragua but belonging to Colombia, is enclosed, with 48 slides (and captions) for your selection.

I'm including this note to share some additional information I discovered in Providencia.

As the article explains, Morgan, the pirate, used Providencia as his port. For years treasure has been sought on and around the island. Two years back the first results of that search came when remains of a ship were found under the sand only 100 yards from the present dock, and a chest was brought up that contained Spanish coins. That is elaborated upon in the article.

What I discovered is that Mrs. Betty Dowd, widow of the crew chief that extracted the chest, has some 40 excellent slides of the item being removed from the water, opened on the shore, and the coins being cleaned and inspected. She let me view the slides and promised that she would make them available to me if you were interested in using one for the cover.

Based on the cover rate stated in last year's Writer's Market, I told her that, if used, she could expect $200. (That was the first question she asked!) Naturally I made no promise for their use, and I explained that, if you were interested, you would have to see at least 20 slides from which to select. I picked the best 20, left her a heavy plastic slide holder, and showed her how to insure and register the mailing to me.

Frankly, I think they are super shots, have never been used before, and would frame the article perfectly. But it's up to you. If interested, let me know, I'll call her, and I can have these in your hands within about a week from that time. No word from you and I'll drop her a thank you note in about a month.

Let me know if I can be of further assistance.

Respectfully,

Gordon Burgett

# Cover Letter Example #8

# Photo Cover Letter

*Purpose*

In this example I've just finished writing an article about Providencia for *The Sightseer*, in response to a query, and am submitting it with this cover letter.

Normally there is no need for a cover to accompany a queried manuscript submission — unless there is something unique or particular to note or add. Here I want to add. That is explained in the first two paragraphs.

*Third Paragraph*

To understand the importance of what I found it is necessary to restate a key point in the article: that Morgan's treasure has been sought since the 1600's on this small island — and that treasure was indeed found within sight of the main pier just two years back!

*Fourth Paragraph*

But I made a discovery of my own. Slides of that treasure being removed exist, they are excellent, and they have never been used. Ideal for the cover! Best yet, I can get them for the editor's review.

*Paragraphs 5-6*

The details. Money. When the editor can get them. How they will be sent.

*Paragraph 7*

On the other hand, there may just be a cover gem in my 48 slides accompanying this letter. Finding Morgan's gold was a miracle — and it was close at hand. So are my slides.

*In Retrospect*

I've sold plenty of photos found during research in just this way, so it works. Editors appreciate it too, though they'd rather not have you bandy about their fees as I had to do here. A cover letter is also a good way to tell where you found the best historical pictures in the texts you consulted, each with the author, title, edition, page number, and photo credit listed.

## Cover Example #9

123 Main Street
Carpinteria, CA 93013
(805) 123-4567
Month 1, Year

Mr. Ira Cyril
Editor, World Business News
7818 Grafton St.
Boston, MA 08000

Dear Mr. Cyril:

Sorry for the two-week delay in getting this article in your hands.

As you recall from our phone conversation about three weeks back, my interview with Cedric Johnstone was postponed because of an urgent trip he had to make to China, then Japan, on State Department business.

The interview, held last Tuesday in New York City, was far more informative, though, because of the trip, and I think the article shows that.

In fact, if interested, it opens up the possibility of an intriguing side-bar or box on the growing interest in China about Japan's establish-ment of an automated computer production plant in China itself. Mr. Johnstone gave me some specific facts about this, plus three names I might contact for further information. I'd need about a week to bring it together. Please let me know if you are interested, a preferred length, any specific info desired, and a deadline. Or would this be a better article for a future issue?

As for the article, source validation gladly provided for any of the points made or facts cited.

Let me know if I can be of further assistance.

Respectfully,

Gordon Burgett

# Cover Letter Example #9

# Delayed Submission Cover Letter

*Purpose*

In this case we had queried the editor of *World Business News* and expected to have the copy in his hands in three weeks. But late in the second week our interview with a key person central to the article had to be postponed. We called Mr. Cyril, explained the situation, and asked for a delay until that interview could be completed.

So now we are submitting the final manuscript, plus a cover letter reminding him of our previous telephone call and some information specific to that postponed interview.

*Third Paragraph*

What gives this cover letter extra yardage is found here. Mind you, most would end after the first two paragraphs and a courteous closing. But here we have the possibility of adding to the article being sent (for an additional payment), or even the core of a later article. So we give the information needed about a sidebar — basic facts, some idea of the sources, and when it can be sent. And we leave open the possibility of being asked to send a fuller query about a later article, if the editor is that interested.

*Thoughts*

It is rare that you delay manuscript submissions so this form simply must be made to meet the particular situation. Use common sense. It's just a courtesy letter anyway. Sometimes it opens up additional sales.

## Cover Example #10

123 Main Street
Carpinteria, CA 93013
(805) 123-4567
Month 1, 1985

Ms Mary Ann Farrens
Fiction Editor, Hansun House Publishers
1738 Broadway
New York, NY 10000

Dear Ms Farrens:

I am submitting three chapters and a synopsis of my latest novel, <u>White Gold</u>, as suggested in the current <u>Writer's Market</u>. (My previous three were published by Albany Woods Press, which no longer handles fiction.)

There are three additional factors that might particularly interest you, Ms Farrens, or the Hansun House marketing editor, that would not be apparent from simply reading the text, thus this short cover letter.

First, "white gold" refers to a form of sap from a rare palm tree found only in the Oriente area of Ecuador where the Paushi-Yaco and Chapano Rivers meet. Its curative powers are well known in the medical world, as they were to the northernmost group of Indians conquered by the Incas.

Second, its value tops $3000 a liter. That has drawn to this primitive area at least six groups, really gangs, hell bent on extracting every last ounce for commercial sale. The result is predictable: gang wars have left scores dead in this lawless jungle. At the same time the gangs are wiping out a fierce group of Indians called the Aucas. And the trees themselves, sensitive to excessive tapping, may well be totally eliminated before scientists can get in to save some of the species for planting and cultivation elsewhere.

Third, what I have told you is true. I was a liaison member with a U.N. task force attempting to enter the area to effect just such a preservation. The news of this sap, its nearly miraculous powers on malignancies and growth deformations, and the plight of the palm and those attempting to save it will hit the news soon.

The book, as the chapters show, puts the story into a slightly fictionalized context, to permit a better look at the gangs, about which virtually nothing is otherwise known. But the rest, except the names and a few modifications to protect actual people, is true. It makes super reading because it's so damned tragic.

If you think it merits publication, let me know quickly and I can have the rest of the text in your hands in ten days. Then when the news pops, so do you.

If there are any questions, please write or call.

Respectfully,

Gordon Burgett

# Cover Letter Example #10

# Cover Letter for a Novel

*Purpose*

To tell Ms Farrens why my novel is particularly time-worthy and why some lucky publisher rushing it into print will be in the chips when the subject about which it is written hits the news!

*Paragraphs 1-2*

A quick explanation of why I'm sending a cover letter along with the chapters and synopsis. I also slipped in a plug that I've already had three novels in print.

*Paragraphs 3-6*

Here's the subject and why it will be in the newspapers and on TV — and why, by implication, my book will be hot material for a movie or TV special. Without this rather elaborate background the book's just another hacker's dream, another so many pages in the pile to be read if and when somebody gets to it. And probably to be rejected as being too farfetched — too far from reality yet not far enough to be a *Star Wars*. So I draw a special look by sending it with a special cover letter.

*Paragraph 7*

If Ms Farrens believes the first six paragraphs and likes what she sees in skimming the synopsis and chapters accompanying the letter, she may well ask to see the whole book — today, sent air express! So the book's in print before the news!

*In Retrospect*

It's a good way to get special attention brought to your novel. But you can't fake it. There should be a reason for writing the cover letter, other than your desperation to get into print and get rich.

Incidentally, do you believe that malarky about the rare palm tree sap and its super cures? Sorry. I couldn't even sell that to Hansun House, since they are as fictional as the plot. The only thing that is real is Mary Ann Farrens. She's my step-aunt and a sweet gal. But from Missouri and a school teacher. I couldn't even sell it to Mary Ann, cover letter or not.

# GLOSSARY

**angle.**   An approach to an idea or subject, a point of view, a way of researching a topic and writing about it for print. For example, an article about a professional baseball player as seen by the batboy.

**approach.**   See angle. A way of seeing a topic and writing about it for print.

**assignment.**   An understanding or a contract in which an editor asks a writer to prepare and submit an article or book, often with specific stipulations about length, due date, and payment.

**b/w.**   Black and white photograph. Also b&w.

**flush left, ragged right.**   In this book the margins of the query or cover letter. In flush left, all the margins are lined up evenly, in vertical order. In ragged right, they are irregular on the right.

**go-ahead.**   A positive reply to a query letter telling the writer to prepare and submit the manuscript, that the editor will seriously consider the finished piece for publication. Usually means the work is performed on speculation.

**ms/mss.**   Abbreviations for manuscript and manuscripts. Also MS/MSS.

**package.**   Editors often consider, and buy, manuscripts and illustrations together, as a "package."

**pix.**   Pictures; photos and/or slides.

**proofsheets.** Instead of enlarged photographic prints, the negative strips are laid on a contact sheet and the whole roll is developed, with each photo the same size as the negative.

**reprint.** Once an item has been in print, each time it reappears in print, as is or with few substantive changes, it is called a reprint. Reprint rights and second rights are the same thing. Reprints usually require an accompanying cover letter when submitted for sale.

**rewrites.** Using one article as the base, a rewrite generally includes much of the same contents but deletes or adds information and/or alters the order of the original contents to produce a different article.

**SASE.** Self-addressed, stamped envelope.

**slant.** See angle. A way of seeing or approaching a topic and writing about it for print.

**speculation.** When "writing on speculation" the freelancer writes on the understanding that the editor is not committed to buy the item or pay a fee if it isn't used.

**tearsheets.** Literally, page(s) from a magazine or newspaper containing the writer's printed copy. Copies of the original work are acceptable in this modern age.

# Bibliography

Boggess, Louise, *Article Techniques That Sell.* San Mateo, CA: B & B Press, 1978.

Burgett, Gordon, *How To Sell 75% of Your Freelance Writing.* Carpinteria, CA: Write To Sell, 1984.

Burgett, Gordon, *Ten Sales From One Article Idea: The Process and Correspondence.* Carpinteria, CA: Write To Sell, 1982.

Casewit, Curtis, *How To Write What Sells and How To Sell What You Write.* New York: Macmillan, 1982.

Gunther, Max, *Writing The Modern Magazine Article.* Boston: The Writer, 1976.

Spikol, Art, *Magazine Writing: The Inside Angle.* Cincinnati: Writer's Digest Books, 1981.

*Writer's Market,* current edition. Cincinnati: Writer's Digest Books.

Young, Jordan, *How To Become a Successful Freelance Writer.* Anaheim, CA: Moonstone Press, 1983.

Zobel, Louise, *The Travel Writer's Handbook.* Cincinnati: Writer's Digest Books, 1984.

# Index

# Also available from
# COMMUNICATION UNLIMITED

## BOOKS

| Title | Price |
|---|---|
| Query Letters/Cover Letters (paper) | $ 9.95 |
| Query Letters/Cover Letters (cloth) | 12.95 |
| Speaking For Money (paper) | 9.95 |
| Speaking For Money (cloth) | 12.95 |
| How To Sell 75% of Your Freelance Writing (paper) | 9.95 |
| How To Sell 75% of Your Freelance Writing (cloth) | 12.95 |
| Ten Sales From One Article Idea | 7.95 |

## TAPES
### (Series, with workbooks)

| | |
|---|---|
| How To Sell 75% of Your Freelance Writing (4 60-minute tapes) | 49.95 |
| Writing Travel Articles That Sell (3 tapes) | 39.95 |
| Writing Comedy Greeting Cards That Sell (2 tapes) | 24.95 |
| How To Write or Speak an Idea Into a Windfall (3 tapes) | 39.95 |
| How To Set Up and Market Your Own Seminar (3 tapes) | 39.95 |

### (Single 60-minute tapes)

| | |
|---|---|
| Finding Ideas for Articles That Sell | 9.95 |
| Research: Finding Facts, Quotes, and Anecdotes | 9.95 |
| How To Write Query Letters That Sell Articles/Books | 9.95 |
| Back-of-the-Room Sales | 9.95 |
| Producing and Selling Your Audio Cassettes | 9.95 |
| Selling Your Product (and Others') by Mail Order | 9.95 |
| Creating, Selling, and Using Your Own Mailing List | 9.95 |

**Tax:** California residents, add 6% sales tax
**Shipping:** $1, first book, tape, or series; 50 cents each additional
$2.50 maximum

## COMMUNICATION UNLIMITED
P.O. Box 1001
Carpinteria, CA 93013